Student Strategy Guide

_____

Write Your Name Here

WELCOME!

This Student Strategy Guide is provided as a supplement to the instructional portion of the Strategies for Success ACT/SAT Preparation course. Please take time to study your Student Strategy Guide. This book represents thousands of hours of research on what works on standardized tests. You can't expect to be successful if you have not mastered these strategies. To really improve your scores you should plan on at least 5 to 10 hours of practicing these strategies on real exam questions.

ONLINE REFERRALS

Start thinking about friends you know who you think would be interested in an ACT/SAT prep course. Our guest reward policy is a unique way to benefit both you and your friends. You can make referrals to us in the following ways:

1. Online at 4SatPrep.com under contact us.

2. Fill out a referral sheet in class.

3. Text your contacts to 843.509.8690

CLASS SCHEDULE FLYER

If you would like to invite someone to the next session ask your instructor for brochures or a flyer. Feel free to make copies of the flyer to give to people you know. Friends don't let friends take boring prep courses!

©Jantzi Test Prep, Inc.
4actprep.com

NOTES

©Jantzi Test Prep, Inc.
4actprep.com

HOW THE COURSE WORKS

100% MONEY BACK GUARANTEE

Jantzi Test Prep has stood by its money back guarantee for over 25 years. Our policy is simple: If we haven't helped your child improve, we haven't earned your money! Since 1987, we have successfully prepared tens of thousands of students achieving a 98% success rate. However, if a student's scores don't improve we will refund the tuition. All a student has to do is:

1. Attend all 12 hours of Strategies for Success in consecutive sessions and check in each time.
2. Complete all work in the Student Strategy Guide (SSG) before the exam.
3. Take the exam within 30 days of the last session attended.

If neither Math nor Reading nor Writing/English nor Science (ACT) scores increase from your best previous individual section scores, Jantzi Test Prep will gladly refund the full tuition. Submit refund requests within 60 days of the test date including the score report. After scores, attendance, and all work in the SSG is verified, a refund will be issued.

COURSE REPETITION POLICY

All students may repeat any or all sessions of STRATEGIES FOR SUCCESS as many times as they choose, at any location,**AT NO ADDITIONAL CHARGE**. Graduates are encouraged to do this in order to receive maximum benefit from the course.Some students have raised their scores hundreds of points this way.

CLASS SCHEDULING

Every effort has been made to set class dates and times to be as convenient as possible for all students. The class schedule has been set in advance to help you plan ahead. Sometimes events arise that make it impossible to attend a session. If this occurs, students may make up the session at another location or during a future course at any location. For this reason, no individual make-up sessions will be offered. Remember, the score increase guarantee does not apply until a student has attended all six sessionsconsecutively.

GUEST POLICY

We appreciate your referrals. One of the benefits of our program is the **FREE** guest policy. Any student may attend one two-hour session **FREE**. When you bring a guest to class, you earn $20.00 This is our way of thanking you for bringing your friends to visit. Invite people you know from school, church and other extra-curricular activities.

NO TAPING POLICY

No audio or videotaping is allowed in class. Cell phones should be powered off while present.

©Jantzi Test Prep, Inc.
4actprep.com

NOTES

©Jantzi Test Prep, Inc.
4actprep.com

CLASS EXPECTATIONS

1. Plan your schedule (work, activities, etc.) in advance for the week, so you will be able to attend all class sessions.

2. Come with an open mind. You will be taught things that may contradict your current practices.

3. Arrive 10 minutes before class and review the previous session.

4. Arrive prepared. Bring something to write with, class materials and your homework.

5. Get involved. Ask questions; raise your hand to answer.

6. Work hard and have fun. Learning and enjoyment are not mutually exclusive.

7. Sign in each night and wear your nametag.

8. We encourage you to tell others about our program. Any student may come as a first-time guest to any session the first time FREE.

9. Keep up with your Student Strategy Guide and write your name inside the front cover There will be a $30.00 charge for replacement of a lost Student Strategy Guide.

10. You will be responsible for completing homework assignments on your own. However, should you have trouble with the homework or with any of the strategies we teach, we encourage you to seek extra help from your instructor before or after class.

11. You must bring a calculator to the Math sessions.

12. Download a copy of a free practice test from the web immediately (instructions on next page).

©Jantzi Test Prep, Inc.
4actprep.com

NOTES

©Jantzi Test Prep, Inc.
4actprep.com

HOW TO PRINT A PRACTICE SAT

1. Go to collegeboard.org and select SAT at the top.

2. Click in the box labeled Practice in the middle of the page towards the bottom.

3. Go to left margin and click on SAT Practice Tests under Practice.

4. Go to the middle of the page and click on SAT Practice Test Answer Sheet and just below that SAT: Practice Test 1. Notice there are other tests below for more practice later.

5. Print both.

HOW TO PRINT A PRACTICE ACT

1. Go to ACTStudent.org.

2. Click on Test Prep at the top left on the navigation bar.

3. Under Test Prep in the middle of the page, click on *Preparing for the ACT* to print the sample test.

4. Print.

©Jantzi Test Prep, Inc.
4actprep.com

NOTES

©Jantzi Test Prep, Inc.
4actprep.com

HOW SHOULD I PRACTICE FOR STANDARDIZED TESTS?

1. The saying "practice makes perfect is not accurate. Practice does not make perfect – it makes permanent. If you do things wrong over and over, you get good at doing things wrong. This is why you signed up for a prep course – so you can learn the right way to do the problems. Therefore, follow these directions exactly.

2. **After** you learn the strategies, practice taking tests under exam-type conditions.
   - Most importantly, take previously administered tests. You must use REAL Exam questions. You can print one(see pg. 6) or go to Amazon.com and order the latest edition of the Official SAT Study Guide **2016** for about $17, or The REAL ACT Prep Guide **Third Edition** for $21.
   - Find an empty classroom at school after hours – you won't be taking the real test at your kitchen table, so you should get used to the testing environment.
   - Make sure you bring a watch. You can buy a cheap one for 10 dollars at Wal-Mart. We don't trust the clock on the wall to be working, let alone accurate!
   - Budget your time: decide how many questions you are going to do, and do them! Remember, you don't have to do all of the questions.
   - Make sure you're properly motivated (what reward will you get when you're done?).
   - Obviously, do not use iPods or cell phones.

3. Do one section at a time with no break. Use a pencil and write on the <u>preparation booklet</u> (from page 6) lightly so you can erase it later and redo the same section in a week or two to see if you make the same mistakes.

4. Get up and take a five-minute break.

5. Check your answers, and go over what you got wrong. There is only **one** way to do this. You read the question (if it's a reading passage, you then read the story), then you read your answer, then you read the right answer. Rinse and repeat. This is the part where I usually grab a student and threaten them with imminent violence. This part is a huge deal! No one wants to focus on their mistakes. But if you don't, you are doomed to repeat them. Look at the dumb answer you put down. Now, what's wrong with it? You've got to beat this into your head! If you don't know, grab another student and make them show you how to do it. Why is their answer better? Go over and over this to see what you did wrong. Look for any patterns in your mistakes. If it's a math problem, successfully rework the problem. Don't just say: "I know what I did wrong."

6. Keep taking practice tests to work up your endurance to the point where you can do two or three sections consecutively without a break. Remember, the actual exams are much longer!

©Jantzi Test Prep, Inc.
4actprep.com

NOTES

©Jantzi Test Prep, Inc.
4actprep.com

CLASS TOPIC SCHEDULE

1. How to Attack Standardized Tests
   - Test-Taking Strategies
   - Time-Saving Techniques

2. How to Attack Standardized Tests
   - Process of Elimination Skills
   - Vocabulary Development

3. How to Attack the Reading Sections
   - Passage Questions
   - Evidenced Based Reading

4. How to Attack the English and Language Sections
   - Multiple Choice Grammar Questions
   - Usage/Mechanics
   - Rhetorical Skills

5. How to Attack the Math Section
   - Student-Produced Response Questions
   - Multiple Choice Questions

6. How to Attack the Math Section
   - Mathematics Review
   - Mathematics Strategies
   - Test Day Preparation

©Jantzi Test Prep, Inc.
4actprep.com

NOTES

©Jantzi Test Prep, Inc.
4actprep.com

WHAT YOU SHOULD KNOW ABOUT THE ACT?

1. **What is the format of the ACT?**
   A. Three-hour exam without the Writing option
   B. Four sections: English section, Math section, Reading section, and Science section

2. **How is the ACT scored?**
   A. Omitted responses neither add to nor detract from your score
   B. The number of questions you get right is your raw score which is then converted to a scaled score (0-36).
   C. Once a student achieves a raw score of 30 almost every additional question they get right results in a 1 point increase in their scaled score!

3. **How are ACT scores used?**
   A. It is a nationwide academic litmus test designed to be a predictor of college success or failure
   B. Its not an IQ Test
   C. Measures achievement
   D. Is used in conjunction with high school grades to make admissions decisions for post-secondary institutions
   E. Minimum ACT scores are easy to program into admission computers at colleges
   F. High scores are used in appropriating the millions of dollars in financial aid available

4. **How can students get ready for the ACT?**
   A. Read every challenging literary work you can find
   B. Practice taking real ACTs in as close to a test - like environment as possible
   C. Learn test-taking strategies specific to the ACT

5. **What is Strategies for Success?**

   A. A fun, convenient, cost-effective program for students who wish to improve scores

   B. Students enjoy the classes and are excited about learning how to best attack problems

   C. Taught in convenient locations and is scheduled to accommodate extracurricular activities

©Jantzi Test Prep, Inc.
4actprep.com

NOTES

WHAT YOU SHOULD KNOW ABOUT THE SAT

1. What is the SAT?
   A. Three-hour, 50 minute exam (including the optional 50 minute essay)
   B. Four sections:
      a. Reading test
      b. Writing and Language test
      c. No calculator Math test
      d. Calculator allowed Math test
   C. Not an IQ Test
      1. Designed to be a predictor of college success or failure
      2. Measures reasoning ability
      3. The SAT is used in conjunction with high school grades to make admissions decisions for post-secondary institutions
      4. Can cause irreparable damage to confidence of low-scoring students

2. How is the New SAT scored?
   A. 154 questions in the three sections (Reading, Writing and Language, Math,) are converted to a scaled score
   B. The maximum score is 1600 and the minimum scaled score is 400
   C. All students begin with 400 points (200 Math/200 Reading and Writing and Language)

3. How are SAT scores used?
   A. It is a nationwide academic litmus test
   B. Minimal SAT scores are easy to program into admissions computers at colleges
   C. High scores are instrumental in appropriating the millions of dollars in financial aid available

4. How can students get ready for the SAT?
   A. Practice taking real SATs in as close to a test-like environment as possible
   B. Learn test-taking strategies specific to the SAT

5. What is *Strategies for Success*?
   A. The most comprehensive SAT/PSAT preparation course available
   B. 12 hours of instruction on how to maximize student performance
   C. A fun, convenient, cost-effective program for students who wish to improve scores
      1. Students enjoy the classes and are excited about learning how to best attack problems
      2. **SFS** is taught at a convenient location and is scheduled to accommodate students' extracurricular activities
      3. Score improvement guaranteed or your money back!
      4. Tuition is $495.00, which includes all materials

©Jantzi Test Prep, Inc.
4actprep.com

NOTES

©Jantzi Test Prep, Inc.
4actprep.com

ACT REGISTRATION RECOMMENDATIONS

To register for the ACT, you go to actstudent.org. You will need to create a student account. **Use a password you're going remember** - it's a nightmare when you can't remember your password. You can't print your admission ticket if you can't log in!

Test Information Release (TIR)

One way we learn is from our mistakes. After you take a test, your teacher returns it to you to show you the incorrect answers, and then they go over it with you. This is essential for learning how to improve. However, the ACT does not provide feedback unless you pay for this service. You have to order the Test Information Release (TIR) You can do this when you register, or at any time within **3 months** after the test date. Note that reports take about 4 weeks to get, so you may not receive yours before the next test date. So you should order it as early as possible - preferably when you register. This service is invaluable to identifying problem areas. Our tutors can look at the (TIR) and very quickly diagnose what is wrong and recommend the prescription to fix it. You will also be able to practice on problem areas.

The (TIR) provides a copy of the ACT you took, including all test questions, your answers, the correct answers. If you are taking the test multiple times, this affords you the opportunity to efficiently improve your scores. (Please note the (TIR) is not available for every test date. It is usually available for the **December, April,** and **June** test dates.)

Late or Standby Registrations:

Most people sign up for the ACT at least five weeks in advance. If you wait too long to sign up, you have to pay an additional late fee of $25. But what happens when you forget to register in time or decide at the last minute to take it again? That is what standby registration is for. There is a 2 week period immediately after late registration when you can do this online. On the day of the exam you must present your standby ticket, photo ID, and you are not guaranteed a seat. You do get your money back if they deny you.

As of January 2016, the fees are:

Regular Fee ACT Test.........$39.50
With Writing......................$56.50
Late Registration $25
Standby Registration..........$49
TIR......................................$20

©Jantzi Test Prep, Inc.
4actprep.com

NOTES

©Jantzi Test Prep, Inc.
4actprep.com

SAT REGISTRATION RECOMMENDATIONS

To register for the SAT, you go to sat.collegeboard.org. You'll need to create a student account. **Use a password you're going remember** – it's a nightmare when you can't remember your password. You can't print your admission ticket if you can't log in!

SAT Question and Answer Service (QAS) $18:

One way we learn is from our mistakes. After you take a test, your teacher returns it to you to show you the incorrect answers, and then they go over it with you. This is essential for learning how to improve. However, the SAT does not provide feedback unless you pay for this service. You have to order Question and Answer Service (QAS). You can do this when you register, or at any time within five months after the test date. Note that QAS reports take a while (6-8 weeks) to send, so you may not receive yours before the next SAT test date. You should order as early as possible. This service is invaluable to identifying problem areas. **Our tutors can look at the QAS and very quickly diagnose what's wrong – and make the prescription for fixing it.** You, as the student, will have more time to practice on problem areas.

The QAS provides a copy of the SAT you took, including all test questions, your answers, the correct answers and the level of difficulty for each question. If you are taking the SAT multiple times, this affords you the opportunity to efficiently improve your scores. (Please note the QAS is not available for every test date. It is usually available for the October, January, and May test dates.)

Remember, when you sign up online, there is a difference between the QAS and the SAS. The SAS (Student Answer Service) does not provide the questions from the test, only the answers. This will not be as useful as the QAS. We highly recommend you spend the extra money and order the QAS, because it is the better choice to significantly boost your score.

Waitlist Registration $46:

Most people sign up for the SAT at least five weeks in advance. If you wait too long to sign up, you have to pay an additional late fee of $26. But what happens when you forget to register in time or decide at the last minute you need to take another SAT? That's what waitlist registration is for. It is a way to take the SAT by just <u>showing up</u> at the test center. Most people do not know you can do this. Waitlisting actually works well.

Here is how you do it:
- Pre-print the registration form online and have it already filled out.
- Show up at the test site. (Make sure the test is being given at that school on that date.)
- Show up 15 minutes early and simply pay by personal check or money order (no cash or credit cards). As of January 2016, the fees are:

Regular Fee SAT I Test ......w/o Essay... $43	= $43
Regular Fee SAT I Test .....w/ Essay......$54.50	= $54.50
Late Registration $28	$54.50 + $28 = $82.50
or	
Waitlist Registration.........................$46	$54.50 + $43 = $97.50

©Jantzi Test Prep, Inc.
4actprep.com

NOTES

©Jantzi Test Prep, Inc.
4actprep.com

SAT	ACT

> Given: No one test will ever be 100% accurate at predicting a student's potential to be successful in college.

SAT	ACT
Total score 400-1600 (10 – 40 scaled for each section)	Scaled score 1-36
No penalty for guessing	No penalty for guessing
Achievement test – measures a student's learning to date	Achievement test – measures a student's learning to date
Reading – 52 questions, 65 min Writing and Language – 44 questions, 35 min No Calculator Math – 20 questions, 25 min Calculator Math – 38 questions, 55 min Essay – 50 min (optional)	English -75 questions, 45 min Math - 60 questions, 60 min Reading - 40 questions, 35 min Science - 40 questions, 35 min Essay – 30 min (optional)
Math purportedly tests more real-life skills	Tests higher-level math, including Trigonometry
All questions have 4 multiple choice answers except for Student Produced Response questions	4 multiple choice answers per section except for math which has 5
7 times a year – Oct/Nov/Dec/Jan/Mar/May/June	6 times a year – Sept/Oct/Dec/Feb/Apr/June
Students *should* continue to take it if they performed well on the PSAT	Most students *should* take it at least twice
3 hours, 50 minutes of testing (including optional Essay)	3 hours, 25 minutes of testing (including optional Writing)

©Jantzi Test Prep, Inc.
4actprep.com

NOTES

©Jantzi Test Prep, Inc.
4actprep.com

WHEN SHOULD I TAKE THE ACT/SAT? (CP)

SCHOOL YEAR	EXAM DATE	EXAM TYPE	SCALED SCORE			
			READING +	'RITING' +	'RITHMETIC' =	COMBINED
SOPH	OCTOBER	PSAT	52	50	53	155
SOPH	MARCH / MAY	SAT	500	510	520	1530
JUNIOR	OCTOBER	PSAT	54	53	55	162
JUNIOR	DECEMBER / JANUARY	SAT	550	540	560	1650
JUNIOR	MARCH / MAY	SAT	580	550	530	1660
SENIOR	SEPTEMBER	ACT	READING 25	ENGLISH 24	MATH 23	SCIENCE 23 ⇨ (24)
SENIOR	OCTOBER	SAT	590	570	510/560*	1720

*REPORTED TO COLLEGES

©Jantzi Test Prep, Inc.
4actprep.com

NOTES

©Jantzi Test Prep, Inc.
4actprep.com

TEST-TAKING STRATEGIES

©Jantzi Test Prep, Inc.
4actprep.com

NOTES

©Jantzi Test Prep, Inc.
4actprep.com

TEST-TAKING STRATEGIES

1. **You only have to be smart for 60 minutes maximum (math). Otherwise it's only 35-45 minutes for the other 3 sections.**

2. **Make sure your answer is being recorded in the appropriate space.** Use the "assembly line" method instead of "playing ping-pong."

   Avoid Ping Pong: "Ping-ponging" is plotting the answers as you go on the answer sheet, going back and forth between the answer sheet and test booklet.

   Use Assembly Line: Record all of your answers in the question booklet first. Then, when you finish each page, transfer the answers from the booklet to the answer sheet. BUT, don't forget to reserve enough time to transfer answers from the last page of a section to the answer sheet. If necessary, use ping-pong when you're running out of time in the last couple of minutes of the test. This saves you 14 minutes and 20 seconds! (215Q x 4 seconds)

3. **Dull pencils bubble faster and you will not get points for your bubble aesthetics.**

4. **Don't skip around. Start with the easy questions, and work straight through.**

5. **How many questions should you answer?** If your goal is only a 1000 on the SAT or 21 on the ACT, you should only attempt the easiest 80% of the problems.

6. **Read carefully (annul can be read as annual!).** You never save time by reading too fast! You should read as fast as you can, not as fast as you can't.

7. **Hey buddy buy a watch!** You don't want to run out of time to do all the problems that you have decided to attempt in a section, so make sure you monitor how much time you spend on the questions, especially the easy ones. Remember, the clock is your friend.

8. **Sometimes when you get nervous about something, you should ask yourself what** is the **worst thing that could happen to me if I screw this up?** Remember, you can retake the exam. No matter what happens, Jantzi, your parents and your friends will still love you. During the exam, if you get nervous take slow deep breaths. If you get tired, take a 20 second mental vacation. Think of something enjoyable for a brief period, this will help you get your focus back.

9. **Never give up on your memory!** Never believe that you've completely forgot how to do a problem.

©Jantzi Test Prep, Inc.
4actprep.com

NOTES

©Jantzi Test Prep, Inc.
4actprep.com

DIFFERENCES IN FORMAT OF ACT AND SAT I

SAT I

154 Questions / 3 hours, 50 minutes
5 SECTIONS (Including Optional Essay)

ACT

215 Questions / 3 hours, 25 minutes
5 SECTIONS (Including Optional Writing)

SECTIONS (*Always* in this order)

1. 65 min Reading (52)
2. 35 min Writing and Language (44)
3. 25 min Math No Calculator (20)
4. 55 min Math Calculator (38)
5. 50 min Essay (Essay)

SECTIONS (*Always* in this order)

1. 45 min English (75) 4 choices
2. 60 min Math (60) 5 choices
3. 35 min Reading (40) 4 choices
4. 35 min Science (40) 4 choices
5. 30 min Writing (optional)

EVIDENCED BASED READING
21 Questions Analysis in Science
21 Questions Analysis in History/Social Studies
10 Dual Passage (Passage 1/ Passage 2)

52 QUESTIONS / 65 MINUTES

WRITING AND LANGUAGE

4 Passages of 11 Questions each
Topics: Career Related, Humanities, History/Social Studies/ and Science

44 QUESTIONS / 35 MINUTES

MATH
45 Regular Multiple Choice (RMC)
13 Student Produced Response (SPR)

58 QUESTIONS / 80 MINUTES

ENGLISH
40 Usage/Mechanics
35 Rhetorical Skills

75 QUESTIONS / 45 MINUTES

MATH
24 Pre-Algebra/Elementary Algebra
18 Intermed. Algebra/Coordinate Geometry
18 Plane Geometry/Trigonometry

60 QUESTION / 60 MINUTES

READING
20 Social Studies/Sciences
20 Arts/Literature

40 QUESTIONS / 35 MINUTES

SCIENCE
40 Science Reasoning

40 QUESTIONS / 35 MINUTES

©Jantzi Test Prep, Inc.
4actprep.com

NOTES

©Jantzi Test Prep, Inc.
4actprep.com

GENERAL PSAT INFO

Who takes it: All CP, Honors, or AP students in 9-12 grades planning to go to a four-year college. Also seniors who have never taken an SAT before can take the PSAT to give them an idea of how they would do on the SAT.

When/Where: The PSAT is given once a year during the third week of October. Unlike the SAT, it can be given during the school day (Tuesday) or on a Saturday at your school.

What/Why: The PSAT is a low-cost practice SAT. It will acquaint you with the format and question types on the SAT. It will also allow you a great opportunity to practice without fear of a bad score being reported to colleges. Only your 11th grade PSAT score counts as the NMSQT (National Merit Scholars Qualifying Test). A student usually needs a selection index of 210 or more to qualify. Becoming a merit scholar is a great admissions tool, and it almost guarantees you some money.

Registration for the PSAT is $11.00 and is held in guidance during September. The PSAT is comprised of old SAT questions, so preparation for both exams is identical.

Reasons to take the PSAT

1.   ***To earn scholarships and academic recognition.*** By taking the test, juniors may be eligible to enter the National Merit Scholarship Corporation's scholarship competitions, as well as programs that give special recognition to high-achieving Hispanic and African-American students.

2.   ***To practice taking standardized tests like the SAT.*** On average, those who take the PSAT earn higher scores on the SAT than those who don't. One reason: The tests have the same formats, directions, sample questions, and question types. The PSAT also provides free feedback on the test. The SAT does not do this. They charge you for a copy of the test questions and answers. This is called the Student Question and Answer Service and costs $12.

3.   ***To begin the college search.*** The Student Search Service gives PSAT test-takers the option to voluntarily place their names in a pool of college-bound students interested in receiving admission and financial aid information from certified colleges, universities and scholarship agencies.

4.   ***To see how one's academic skills compare with those of other college students.*** PSAT test results will give most students their first chance to see how their skills compare with those of others planning to go to college.

5.   ***To help direct a learning plan for high school.*** Test results in the PSAT Score Report give students feedback on their college-related verbal, math and writing skills. Students can use this information to fine-tune learning plans, including appropriate course selections that will get them ready for college-level work.

6.   ***PSAT scores are used for identification*** of students for AP and/or Honors classes and to identify students for the many opportunities that come through guidance.

7.   ***PSAT and ACT Plan scores are compared*** by guidance counselors in order to advise students as to which test they should concentrate on during their junior and senior years. This saves students time and money.

©Jantzi Test Prep, Inc.
4actprep.com

NOTES

©Jantzi Test Prep, Inc.
4actprep.com

GUESS WHO HAS A HIGHER SCORE
OR
IT'S GOOD TO BE POE!

Choices per ? Eliminated	# of Hard Questions	Hard ?s Answered		Raw Points		Points Gained	
		Right	Wrong	Earned	Lost	Raw	Scaled
0	60*	12			-12	0	
1			45	+15		+3.75	30
2	60	20		+20	-10		90
3	60				-7.5	+22.5	200
4	60			+60	-0		

* There are a total of _____ questions on the SAT. For the purpose of this chart we designated 60 as the number of hard questions on the SAT. This leaves us with 110 questions that most students could solve for the answer. They would not necessarily need to use _____.

©Jantzi Test Prep, Inc.
4actprep.com

NOTES

©Jantzi Test Prep, Inc.
4actprep.com

READING

STRATEGIES

©Jantzi Test Prep, Inc.
4actprep.com

NOTES

©Jantzi Test Prep, Inc.
4actprep.com

SAT READING - MOST COMMON MISTAKES

1. Not answering the question that was asked.

2. Not reading all of the answer choices.

3. Not reading the whole answer choice.

4. Picking an overstated answer.

5. Expecting a right answer to be perfect.

6. Picking an answer because it's a true statement, not because it best answers the question.

7. Not reading the intro that precedes the passage.

8. Not doing whole passage questions last.

9. Reading too many lines before and after an LRQ.

10. Not reading enough lines before and after an LRQ.

11. Not fully understanding the questions.

©Jantzi Test Prep, Inc.
4actprep.com

NOTES

©Jantzi Test Prep, Inc.
4actprep.com

ACT ENGLISH

FORMAT: 75 Questions/45 minutes/5 passages

Usage and Mechanics	40 Q's	Rhetorical Skills	35 Q's
• Punctuation	10 Q's	1. Writing Strategy	12 Q's
• Grammar and Usage	12 Q's	2. Organization	11 Q's
• Sentence Structure	18 Q's	3. Writing Style	12 Q's

1. **You have just over 30 seconds to answer each question.** You get 9 minutes per passage. The only way to develop a good pace is to practice with a watch!

2. **It helps if you cup your hands tightly over your ears while you read the passage in a whisper.**

3. **Beware of the box!** The hardest questions have a small box around the question number, and/or don't have no change as the first choice. The only time you would just guess blindly on these would be at the end of the English section if you're running out of time. (pg 298 # 37)

4. **Use the two finger method to make sure you're in the right place.** The questions go down the right hand side of the page and refer to the essay on left side. Sometimes you can get confused when a paragraph in the essay ends. If you get confused, you can draw horizontal lines to separate the paragraphs with the questions that pertain to them.

5. **No change is the right answer 25% of the time!** If you read it and nothing jumps out at you, leave it alone.

6. **Don't go into a comma coma.** If it sounds fine without a comma, then don't use a comma!

7. **Make sure you stay tense.** Threatened is the same tense as stationed, made, and indicated. (pg 297 #33)

8. **Don't be redumbdant!** (pg 297 #34)

9. **There, they're, or their? Its or it's?** (pg 299 #41)

10. **"Best conclusion, Most effective transition, or intro"** is asking you for the answer choice that repeats the most information back from the passage. (pg 157 #38)

11. **The most concise answer is the right answer most of the time.** If it sounds just as good without a piece of information then you don't need it. (pg 299 #43)

12. **Read carefully (annul can be read as annual!).** You never save time by reading too fast! You should read as fast as you can, not as fast as you can't.

13. **Before you attempt the last problem before time runs out,** bubble in a guess for all of the other remaining problems.

NOTES

©Jantzi Test Prep, Inc.
4actprep.com

ACT MATH

FORMAT: 60 Q's/60 minutes (32 - 34 Alg. Q's/ 22 - 24 Geom. Q's/ 4 Trig. Q's)

1. **Memorize all the formulas and terms.** Lucky for you, Jantzi has most of them in this Student Strategy Guide. (pg 175 #46)

2. **The only math problems you need to practice on are in the Real ACT red book.**

3. **Read Carefully.** This exam is not about science, math, or whatever they say it is. It's about READING! Make sure you circle important terms like NOT and EXCEPT. (pg 166 #12) Beware of trick questions. (pg 174 #41)

4. **You get one minute per question here.** If you only attempt 50, you get 72 seconds per.

5. **Consider the answer choices before you start working out the problem.** (pg 172 #35)

6. **Diagrams are DTS.** (pg 170 #28) If there is no diagram, draw one. Make sure you have enough room to draw a large enough diagram, and do a good job! (pg 173 #37)

7. **If you are going to work the problem, don't skip steps.** Workout the problem all the way through and write all over the booklet. (pg 165 #8)

8. **If you fall behind, don't hang around.** Give up trying to find the right answer and just eliminate the wrong ones and guess, then move on. (pg 174 #45)

9. **Always convert fractions and percents to decimals with your calculator.** Now check your calculator answer to see if it looks correct. (pg 174 #42 & #44) (pg 166 #11)

10. **Use the substitute principal when there is a variable present.** Don't use numbers that are already in the problem. Use small positive integers unless it tells you not to. (pg 172 #32 & #34)

11. **Play the high low game with the answer choices.** (pg 168 #20)

12. **On hard questions if the first answer looks obvious, it's wrong.** (pg 176 #52)

13. **Pick up a shoe for God's sake!** Don't quit or just assume you don't know how to do it. (pg 164 #4)

14. **Cannot be determined is the lazy way out, and is almost always wrong.** (pg 173 #39)

15. **When two or more answers are similar, the right answer is usually one of them.** (pg 165 #5 & pg 170 #26)

16. **Before you attempt the last problem before time runs out, bubble in a guess for all of the other remaining problems.**

©Jantzi Test Prep, Inc.
4actprep.com

NOTES

©Jantzi Test Prep, Inc.
4actprep.com

ACT READING

FORMAT: 40 Questions/35 minutes/4 passages

Prose - This a narrative that tells a story. You could be asked to interpret a character's feelings, emotions or motives. You need to read between the lines here.

Humanities - The humanities section is based on a passage taken from a memoir or personal essays about architecture, art, dance, ethics, film, language, literary criticism, music, philosophy, radio, television, or theater. The humanities passages are about real people or events. This means that there will still be many facts that you will need to pay attention to, but these passages can also include the author's opinions.

Social Science - The questions are based on writings about anthropology, archaeology, business, economics, education, geography, history, political science, psychology, or sociology. The passages are generally a discussion of research, as opposed to experimentation, and should represent an objective presentation of facts.

Natural Science - The subjects addressed in the natural sciences passage can come from any of the following areas: anatomy, astronomy, biology, botany, chemistry, ecology, geology, medicine, meteorology, microbiology, natural history, physiology, physics, technology, and zoology. The natural science passage can come from any form of scientific writing: a lab report, an article, or textbook. You can expect to see many scientific language, facts, and figures in these types of passages.

1. **Consider not doing one of the four passages.** The four types of passages are: prose fiction, social science, humanities and natural science. Pick the one you hate most and don't do it. If you get all of the other questions right you would get a 27 Reading score! If you are only doing three passages, then the time limit shouldn't be a big problem. If you are targeting a score of 30–36, you need to do all four and you will have nine minutes per passage! This works out to about five minutes to read it and four to answer the questions or vice versa.

2. **Not everything in the passage is pertinent.** So, when you read, keep in mind your objective is to get an overview of what is going on and to know where to find the information you need after you read the questions. (pg 469 #20)

3. **Some students benefit by reading the questions first and then writing the key words in the margin that they want to look for in the passage.** This works well for someone who remembers a little bit about what they said in the story, just not where!

4. **Another way to attack these questions is to do all the line reference questions first.** This is where they tell you the line # to look at in the question. When they mention someone's proper name it automatically makes it line referenced because names are so easy to find because they are capitalized.

©Jantzi Test Prep, Inc.
4actprep.com

NOTES

©Jantzi Test Prep, Inc.
4actprep.com

5. It's possible that reading the passage a little slower might actually make you faster in answering the questions! If you find that you're spending a lot of time looking for information in the passage, (Where they talked about that) you are probably reading the passage too fast.

6. There will always be one question that deals with the first paragraph, so try hard to understand it. If you get lost in the beginning, it will be difficult to figure out what's going on in the passage.

7. Make sure you really understand what they are asking in the questions before you move ahead to the answer choices!

8. Stay with what they say. If they stray, runaway! (pg 469 #13)

9. When you start going back to the passage to find answers, you have to read extremely carefully! Beware of the edges. Many readers miss details if they are in the periphery. (pg 469 #11)

10. Always use process of elimination. If there is one word wrong in the answer choice, it's all wrong! Sometimes if they had changed one word in an answer choice it would have been right! (pg187 #36 Choice J) if you replace the word small with large, this answer is correct.

11. If you still can't find any answer, use common sense. Don't waste too much time on any one question.

12. Often after you have eliminated some wrong answers you will have it down to 2 choices. Instead of trying to figure out which one is right, pick one of them and try to prove it wrong. If you can't prove it wrong, its right!

13. Before you attempt the last problem before time runs out, bubble in a guess for all of the other remaining problems.

©Jantzi Test Prep, Inc.
4actprep.com

NOTES

©Jantzi Test Prep, Inc.
4actprep.com

ACT SCIENCE

FORMAT: 40 Questions/35 Minutes

1. Time is usually an issue here.

2. There are almost always seven passages on the science, but I want you to check as soon as you begin this section. If there are only six it will change the pace you need to follow.

3. Remember it is still a reading test. They still call them passages, not labs or experiments.

4. Don't let words you are unfamiliar with scare you.   (Flood basalt plateau pg 188)

5. Not everything in the passage is pertinent. So when you scan the passage, keep in mind your objective is to get an overview of what is going on and to know where to find the information you need after you read the questions. Don't spend time analyzing charts and tables because you will have to look at them very carefully again anyway.

6. There are two types of information: Words (pg 198 chimney efficiency) or Figures, tables and charts (pg 340) or both. (pg 330)

7. As you're reading the questions, always circle words like not, least, most etc.

8. Now carefully read the question and go find where that answer is in the passage. Where should I look? In just one place: based on the data in figure 2, according to table 1, based on the results of activity 2. In more than one place: based on the data in figures 1 and 2, do the results of experiment 2 and the table below support this hypothesis? (pg 337 #25), according to figure 1, (pg 341 #39) but there are two charts here! Anywhere: on the basis of the information given, if the hypothesis made by the scientist in study 3 is correct (pg 189 #6), according to the data provided, based on the passage.

9. How can I keep track of where I am? (pg 474 #4) If question 4 asks you about method 2, you first have to determine which place to get it from - Table 1 or Figure 1. Then do one of the following: draw a line connecting the question and the Table/Figure, circle it, or put your non-writing finger on the one you select now.

10. If they reference a Figure, there might be two parts. (pg 340, #39)

11. What is trending now? Use your scantron (answer sheet) as a straightedge and extend the method 2 line. Now draw the line where 90 m/hr would be. (pg 474 #5)

12. Be at home on the range. The question asks between which depths it increases most, not when it starts its uptake. Also higher is horizontal not vertical! (pg 341 #40)

13. Now, read the choices carefully. If one word is wrong in an answer, its wrong! (pg 187 #33)

14. If you can't understand the Figure, Table, graph, or passage - use common sense. What the heck do you think will happen to a plant's overall mass when salt is increased to the roots? Salt kills plants! Or what happens to things as you increase their temperature? Hint - they expand.

15. Before you attempt the last problem before time runs out, bubble in a guess for all of the other remaining problems.

©Jantzi Test Prep, Inc.
4actprep.com

NOTES

©Jantzi Test Prep, Inc.
4actprep.com

WRITING

STRATEGIES

©Jantzi Test Prep, Inc.
4actprep.com

NOTES

©Jantzi Test Prep, Inc.
4actprep.com

ACT WRITING SECTION - ESSAY

What will I have to write about?

You will have to read a prompt that requires you to take a position about something related to high school life and then support it. You should make sure to use examples to support your position. If you don't write about the topic they give you, you will receive a score of 0.

How long does the essay have to be?

You only have 30 minutes to write the essay. Almost everyone agrees that longer essays will receive a higher score. A good rule of thumb would be at least 2 pages. Much more than that will not help.

How will they grade the essay?

Two readers will give you a score from 1-6 on the essay, with 6 being the highest score. A score of 4 or higher is considered adequate. The readers are looking for the following things:

1. Content: Choose a position (don't waffle!) and support it with examples. Use logical reasoning to demonstrate how the examples prove your position is the correct one.
   Try to think of yourself as a lawyer presenting a case to a jury. Your goal is to sell your argument..and to tell them why the other side is wrong! Be sure to acknowledge opposing ideas, but still remain firm in your own opinion.
2. Organization: Focus on the question asked and organize your paper so that one idea flows into the next.
3. Vocabulary: Be concise and precise.
4. Sentence structure: Use a variety of sentence structures while writing clearly.
5. Grammar errors: Avoid errors in grammar, usage and mechanics.
6. Neatness always counts.

How should I organize my time?

1. Begin by reading the question carefully. Then formulate a one-sentence summary of the position you plan to take. This will be your thesis sentence. It should contain both a statement of your position and a broad statement of the support for your position. The statement of your position should restate the question asked. It should take you no more than two or three minutes.
2. You will probably not have time to write two drafts or to make a detailed outline, but it is important that you plan what you intend to write before you start. Do so by thinking of two or three examples to support your position. The examples can come from real life, literature, or the classroom. Variety is best.
3. Write your paper by sticking to your plan. You don't have time to change, and what you say is less important than how you say it anyway.

©Jantzi Test Prep, Inc.
4actprep.com

NOTES

©Jantzi Test Prep, Inc.
4actprep.com

WRITING SECTION - ESSAY (CON'T)

How should I organize my essay?

1. Don't write a title.
2. Your first paragraph is your introduction. It should begin broad and become more specific as it progresses. Use the "funnel" approach: ▽
3. **Do not begin with "I", use a 1 wood intead!**
4. **The last sentence of the first paragraph should be your thesis statement.** Your thesis serves as an outline for the rest of the paper. It explains just how you will go about proving that that your position is the correct position. Your thesis should include the two or three examples that you will be explaining in the remaining paragraphs of your essay.
5. Your second paragraph should dive into your first example. Remember to be convincing! Also, use good transition language at the beginning of the paragraph. For example, begin your first sentence with "Another example," or "Also," or "Additionally."
6. Your third and fourth paragraph follows the same pattern as the second.
7. If you have time include a counter argument as paragraph 6.
8. **One would** do well to include a concluding paragraph. This is where you tie all your examples together into a cohesive reason that your position is the correct one. It should be similar to your thesis statement but include some new support for your argument. In other words, conclude in a meaningful and succinct way.

Ten things to remember

1. Write so that the reader hears your voice. Don't be too formal, but avoid colloquialism. In other words, write the essay like it is a formal speech.
2. Write what you know. Pick examples that you feel comfortable talking about.
3. Avoid passive voice. Use "The boy hit the ball" instead of "The ball was hit by the boy." Try not to use the verb "to be" (is, are, was, were, be, being, been).
4. First-person is fine, but avoid using the word "I" too much.
5. Write neatly, even though handwriting is not part of your score. It can be what makes a very good or very bad first impression on the reader.
6. Use words you know. It will hurt more to use a word incorrectly than it will help to use a fancy word. If you don't know how to spell a word, use another one.
7. Indent paragraphs.
8. Practice writing to these prompts. These essays all follow a formula, and you can use the same organizational pattern over and over again.
9. When you do a practice essay, edit it so that you recognize how to improve it. Eventually, you'll just start writing the right way the first time.
10. Write as if you're right. If you're not convinced that your position is correct, the reader will not be either.

©Jantzi Test Prep, Inc.
4actprep.com

NOTES

©Jantzi Test Prep, Inc.
4actprep.com

Thesis sentence

First example (your best)

Second example

Third example

Summary

©Jantzi Test Prep, Inc.
4actprep.com

NOTES

©Jantzi Test Prep, Inc.
4actprep.com

I HAVE NO IDEA WHAT TO WRITE ABOUT!! - (ESSAY)

The essay is the first thing you do when you open your SAT booklet, so already you're going to be nervous before you even read the topic. Once you do, you're probably going to sit there for a few minutes, panicking about what to write about and watching your precious time fly by.

We don't want this to happen to you. And it doesn't have to. There is a very simple trick you can use to keep yourself from wasting too many of your 25 minutes trying to come up with good examples to back your thesis statement:

Know what you're going to write about before you get there!

Wait a second…how can I do that if I haven't read the prompt yet?

Well, the truth is, most of the prompts on the SAT fit roughly into one of twelve categories. If you have examples ready for each of those twelve categories, you'll practically have an outline done before you walk into the testing room! Now, in picking your own personal "arsenal" of examples to plug into your essay, the important thing is to choose those people, events and books you are most familiar with and that genuinely interest you. If you choose wisely and have five of each of these ready to go before the test, you're bound to be able to apply at least a few of them to any given prompt.

1.   **People**

Write down the five historical figures you know most about or that you admire the most. If you can't think of any, you could always use one of mine: Benjamin Franklin, Abraham Lincoln, Martin Luther King, Jr., Nelson Mandela and Mother Theresa.

_____   _____

_____   _____

_____

2.   **Events**

Write down the five historical events or time periods you know most about or that interest you the most. Mine are: World War II, the Civil Rights Movement, the American Revolution, the Information Age and the recent national emergencies, Hurricane Katrina and the BP oil spill.

_____   _____

_____   _____

_____

©Jantzi Test Prep, Inc.
4actprep.com

NOTES

©Jantzi Test Prep, Inc.
4actprep.com

I HAVE NO IDEA WHAT TO WRITE ABOUT!! - (ESSAY)

3.   Books

Write down five books you've read in English class that have been at least halfway interesting to you and that you remember well (ie, can still name the characters, themes and plotline). **Keep in mind that most of the essay graders are high school English teachers, and they love it when you use literature references.** If you can't remember any, here are some suggestions: *Frankenstein, Gulliver's Travels, Pride and Prejudice, The Scarlet Letter, The Great Gatsby, A Farewell to Arms, Animal Farm,* and anything by Shakespeare.

_____   _____

_____   _____

_____

Now, you can't just fill in the blanks and forget about this. If you want to walk into the essay question with confidence, you need to know these people, events and books, and you need to know them *well.*

- ➢ For the people, that means you need a general idea of their biography, accomplishments and historical context: what did their lives change about the world, and how did the world change them?

- ➢ For the events and time periods, you need to know how each of your five fits into history: what caused them, what happened and how did these events impact the country and the world?

- ➢ For the books, you're going to need to know the main characters, basic plotline, themes and historical context: what was the main point, and how did the author get that point across?

Check out the following list of the most commonly used general themes for prompts. See how you could use something from one of your blanks as support for an essay with each of the themes.

Individuality / Creativity   Ethics and Success
Submission to Authority   Technological "Progress"
Motivation and Hardship   Tradition
Collaboration / Independence   Past and future
Justice and Truth   Choices
Sacrifice   Heroism

You should review your list of people, events and books right before you walk into the exam so your ideas are fresh on your mind.

Now, what if there's a prompt that's not listed, or none of the things on your list fit? Think about current events or, worse comes to worse, make up a story about your Uncle Fred that fits the prompt. It's better to have a made-up example that fits your thesis than a fancy literary or historical one that you're not quite sure of.

©Jantzi Test Prep, Inc.
4actprep.com

NOTES

©Jantzi Test Prep, Inc.
4actprep.com

I HAVE NO IDEA WHAT TO WRITE ABOUT!! - (ESSAY)

Practice Worksheet

For each of the general prompt themes listed below, find three examples you could use to support a thesis. Look back on your lists from pages 32-33 for help.

Prompt Theme	Person	Event	Book
Individuality / Creativity			
Submission to Authority			
Motivation and Hardship			
Collaboration / Independence			
Justice and Truth			
Sacrifice			
Ethics and Success			
Technological "Progress"			
Tradition			
Past and future			
Choices			
Heroism			

©Jantzi Test Prep, Inc.
4actprep.com

NOTES

©Jantzi Test Prep, Inc.
4actprep.com

MULTIPLE CHOICE GRAMMAR QUESTIONS

1. **Know what you are looking for.** Each section asks you to look for something different.

Identifying Errors	**Improving Sentences**	**Improving Paragraphs**
- Find errors only	- Find errors and correct	- Answer the question given
- One Sentence	- One Sentence	- Whole paragraph
(~ 18 questions)	(~ 25 questions)	(~ 6 questions)

2. **Don't spend too much time looking for mistakes that aren't there.** Answer choice **E** is always **NO ERROR** on the "Identifying Sentence Errors" part; answer choice **A** is always the sentence written the same way it is in the question – choosing this answer means that there is no error on the "Improving Sentences" part. Don't be afraid to choose it if you can't find any errors and the sentence seems correct to you.

3. **Read the entire sentence in the "Identifying Sentence Errors" and "Improving Sentences" portions.** Sometimes the mistake in the underlined portion has to do with how it relates to the non-underlined portion.

4. **Don't read the paragraph in the "Improving Paragraphs" portion.** This is unnecessary since the questions go in order and are all line-referenced. Simply read the amount necessary to answer the questions as they are presented.

5. **Don't focus just on the underlined portion of the sentences or just the lines referenced in the paragraphs.** Virtually every error on the test deals with how the underlined portion or lines referenced relate to the *SENTENCE AS A WHOLE*, so you have to ask yourself: How does the underlined portion fit with the rest of the sentence?

©Jantzi Test Prep, Inc.
4actprep.com

NOTES

©Jantzi Test Prep, Inc.
4actprep.com

MULTIPLE CHOICE GRAMMAR QUESTIONS (CONT'D)

6. **Know what the possible mistakes are.** The test only focuses on a few different types of writing problems: consistency, logical expression, conciseness, precision and grammar. Be familiar with the different types of errors and focus on looking for these in the sentences. Here are a few general rules and the most common things to look for:

> ➤ **Don't defend a nonsense sentence.** If it seems like it doesn't make sense, then it probably doesn't – even if it uses a lot of SAT-sounding words.
>
> *Example:* Upon disembarking, Columbus appreciated the bounty of the New World's natural treasures as improving his lot in life. No Error.
>
> *Answer:*

> ➤ **Wordiness is bad.** If an answer choice gives you the opportunity to shorten a sentence or combine sentences without changing the meaning or leaving out detail, that's the one you are looking for.
>
> *Example:* He decided to report the larceny to the police himself. According to the incident report, the thief had absconded with a great portion of his master's fortune.
>
> *Rewrite the sentence:* _____
>
> _____
>
> _____

> ➤ **Inactive sentence constructions, particularly passive voice, are bad.** Since these constructions make sentences wordier, it only makes sense that they are incorrect.
>
> *Example:* Jantzi was overwhelmed by his own genius.
>
> *Rewrite as active:* _____
>
> _____

©Jantzi Test Prep, Inc.
4actprep.com

NOTES

©Jantzi Test Prep, Inc.
4actprep.com

MULTIPLE CHOICE GRAMMAR QUESTIONS (CONT'D)

➢ **Look for agreement errors.** This covers a great many types of sentence errors. Make sure your pronouns agree with your nouns, your nouns with your verbs, your nouns with your nouns, and your verbs with your verbs. Pay attention to agreement both in number and tense.

Example: <u>Though believed</u> to be a miserable place <u>to spend</u> a weekend afternoon,
          A   **B**

<u>schools actually</u> can be fun <u>with Jantzi</u> around. <u>No Error.</u>
     C   **D**   **E**

Answer:

Example: <u>We strive</u> to enamor our teacher <u>so that she</u> will award us, even though
           A   **B**

<u>you may not</u> deserve it, with good marks and <u>glowing recommendations for</u> college.
    C   **D**
<u>No Error.</u>
 E

Answer:

Example: <u>An efficient, successful study</u> method is convenient <u>to use</u>, adaptable to
             A   **B**

different subjects, and <u>avoid reliance</u> on <u>last-minute cramming.</u> <u>No Error.</u>
         C   **D**   **E**

Answer:

Example: The plot was doomed to fail <u>because the crooks acted without considering their complexities.</u>

(A) because the crooks acted without considering their complexities.
(B) because the crook acted without considering their complexities
(C) because the crooks act without considering their complexities.
(D) because the crooks acted without considering its complexities
(E) because the crooks acted without considering the complexities.

©Jantzi Test Prep, Inc.
4actprep.com

NOTES

©Jantzi Test Prep, Inc.
4actprep.com

MULTIPLE CHOICE GRAMMAR QUESTIONS (CONT'D)

➤ **Look for run-on sentences or fragments.** Beware of really long sentences separated with a single comma; these could be run-on sentences. Also look for verbs that are missing a subject; these could be fragments.

Example: The earth is round, however, people once believed it was flat.

Rewrite as complete sentence(s): _____

_____

Example: Once I realized how easy it is to write in complete sentences, making sure I have both a subject and a verb, an easy task to perform.

Rewrite as complete sentence(s): _____

_____

➤ **Adverbs end in "-ly."**

Example: He returned as quick as he could when he heard that his mother was ill.

Identify the adverb and write it correctly: _____

➤ **Pay attention to parallel structure.**

Example: Even though British companies offer much more vacation time than Americans, very little difference in productivity occurs.

Rewrite: _____

_____

➤ **Look out for misuse of idioms and awkward constructions.**

Example: When the little boy is tired plus being overly worried, he usually misbehaves.

Rewrite the sentence correctly: _____

_____

©Jantzi Test Prep, Inc.
4actprep.com

NOTES

DECODING WORD MEANING

What do I do when I don't know the meaning of a word?

1. Ask yourself: *Where have I heard this word before?* (Context)

I know you've heard this before, but the best way to find a word meaning is to examine its context. How is the word used? What are they saying in the prior sentence? What about in the sentence after? If the tone of the passage is critical, and the sentence is surrounded by other sentences which are derogatory toward the subject, then the unknown word probably means something negative also.

2. Ask yourself: *Do I know what a part of the word means?*

You don't have to be a Latin scholar to use this strategy! Just break the word into its prefixes, suffixes, and roots. Then try to relate the meaning bit by bit to the whole word. You'll be surprised how many words you can decipher when you examine the possibility that the unknown word might be related to another word you already know.

Example: Periscope
PERI: <u>PERI</u> METER
SCOPE: TELE <u>SCOPE</u>
SCOPE: MICRO <u>SCOPE</u>

Perimeter is the distance around something and *meter* is to measure, so that is the distance part. That means that *peri* must mean **around.** Telescope and microscope are instruments used to look at things, so *scope* means to **look** *Periscope*, then, must be something used to look around. In fact, periscopes are telescopes used on submarines to see above the surface of the water. And, since periscopes can swivel 360 degrees, they allow sailors to **look around** .

3. Ask yourself: *Is it a good witch, a bad witch, or a sandwich?*

No one knows the exact definition of all words. Many times when you're stuck on the meaning of a word, the only thing that registers in your mind is a feeling about that word. These feelings are usually negative or positive. For example, you may not know what *charismatic* means, but you might remember it was used in history class to describe some great leader like Jesus Christ or Abraham Lincoln, etc. This makes it something good and gives you enough information to then eliminate some answer choices and complete the problem.

©Jantzi Test Prep, Inc.
4actprep.com

NOTES

©Jantzi Test Prep, Inc.
4actprep.com

DECODING WORD MEANING – (CON'T)

What do I do when I think I know a word but I still seem way off?

1. **Make sure that you have read the word correctly.** Sometimes you may confuse one word for another simply by misreading. Note these pairs of words which may be easily confused:

   PARITY/PURITY
   COLLEGE/COLLAGE
   CONSCIOUS/CONSCIENCE
   LOOSE/LOSE

2. **Be wary of multiple word meanings,** especially on medium difficulty questions. Consider all possible meanings of a word before giving up on a question. Note the following examples:

WORD	MEANINGS	PART OF SPEECH
AIR	1) What we breathe	Noun
	2) Air your feelings	Verb
FIRE	1) Produces smoke	Noun
	2) Leaves someone jobless	Verb
	3) What you do to a gun	Verb
SUIT	1) Something you wear	Noun
	2) Legal action	Noun
	3) To be agreeable	Verb

©Jantzi Test Prep, Inc.
4actprep.com

NOTES

©Jantzi Test Prep, Inc.
4actprep.com

LATIN FOR DUMMIES: THE RULE OF FOUR OR FIVE LETTERS

1. **What is the rule of four or five letters?**

   If you see four or five letters together in a word that you've seen in some other word, those two words are related.

   For example, everybody knows *benef icial* means something good.
   So why doesn't everybody know that *bene volent* also means something good?

2. **So what parts of this word look familiar?**

   Anthropomorphism = _____ + _____ + _____

3. **What do these roots mean?**

   Anthrop = _____, as in the word _____

   Morph = _____, as in the word _____

   Ism = _____, as in the word _____

4. **So what do we now know about anthropomorphism?**

   _____

5. **So how do I prepare to do this on the SAT? Study the roots in the Student Strategy Guide (pages 48-59) and increase your vocabulary exponentially. Watch this:**

   If you know that a *somnambulist* is a sleepwalker (*somn* = sleep, *ambul* = walk), you also know the following:

somn	*ambul*
Insomnia	Amble
Somnambulism	Perambulate
Somniferous	Circumambulate
Somnolent	Ambulance

©Jantzi Test Prep, Inc.
4actprep.com

NOTES

©Jantzi Test Prep, Inc.
4actprep.com

DECODING WORKSHEET I

DIRECTIONS: Ask yourself what each part of the word means. Then put them together to make a definition.

Example:

Microbiology: small + study of living things = the study of small living things.

1. Periscope: _____ + _____ =

_____

2. Intermediary: _____ + _____ =

_____

3. Antithesis: _____ + _____ =

_____

4. Circumspect: _____ + _____ =

_____

5. Debilitate: _____ + _____ =

_____

6. Extramural: _____ + _____ =

_____

7. Commiserate: _____ + _____ =

_____

8. Somniloquist: _____ + _____ =

_____

©Jantzi Test Prep, Inc.
4actprep.com

NOTES

©Jantzi Test Prep, Inc.
4actprep.com

DECODING WORKSHEET I - (CONT'D)

9. Retrospect: _____ + _____ =

_____

10. Protagonist: _____ + _____ =

_____

11. Complacent: _____ + _____ =

_____

12. Regressive: _____ + _____ =

_____

13. Expatriate: _____ + _____ =

_____

14. Antebellum: _____ + _____ =

_____

15. Misanthrope: _____ + _____ =

_____

16. Introvert: _____ + _____ =

_____

17. Malodorous: _____ + _____ =

_____

18. Philanthropist: _____ + _____ =

_____

©Jantzi Test Prep, Inc.
4actprep.com

NOTES

©Jantzi Test Prep, Inc.
4actprep.com

GOOD WORD / BAD WORD

UNKNOWN WORD	RELATED WORD	GOOD OR BAD?
1. Benefactor		
2. Malevolent		
3. Catatonic		
4. Putrefaction		
5. Philanthropist		
6. Felicity		
7. Bellicose		
8. Shoddy		
9. Misanthrope		
10. Capricious		
11. Lurid		
12. Debase		
13. Banal		
14. Mollify		
15. Eloquent		
16. Indolent		
17. Lurk		
18. Acrid		

©Jantzi Test Prep, Inc.
4actprep.com

NOTES

©Jantzi Test Prep, Inc.
4actprep.com

MULTIPLE WORD MEANINGS

Many times on the SAT, test-makers use a less common usage of a common/easy word to make the question more difficult. Complete this worksheet, filling in the most common meaning first (the one that comes to you first), and then the alternative. In parentheses, write the abbreviation for the part of speech for each word: (v) = verb, (a) = adjective, (n) = noun

	MOST COMMON MEANING	ALTERNATIVE 1	ALTERNATIVE 2
1. Alert	( )	( )	( )
2. Brush	( )	( )	( )
3. Content	( )	( )	( )
4. Discipline	( )	( )	( )
5. Interest	( )	( )	( )
6. Marshal	( )	( )	( )
7. Mean	( )	( )	( )
8. Novel	( )	( )	( )
9. Order	( )	( )	( )
10. Suspect	( )	( )	( )
11. Crane	( )	( )	( )
12. Touch	( )	( )	( )
13. Union	( )	( )	( )
14. Produce	( )	( )	( )
15. Proceeds	( )	( )	( )
16. Train	( )	( )	( )
17. Suit	( )	( )	( )
18. Trust	( )	( )	( )
19. Firm	( )	( )	( )
20. Police	( )	( )	( )

©Jantzi Test Prep, Inc.
4actprep.com

NOTES

©Jantzi Test Prep, Inc.
4actprep.com

DECODING WORSHEET II:

PRACTICE MAKES PREFIX

DIRECTIONS: Try to define as many of these as you can by yourself. **Then** get a dictionary to finish. Look up the words that start with the prefix you're working on, and ask yourself what they all have in common in terms of meaning. Then write the meaning and list two other words that are examples of the prefix's meaning.

PREFIX	MEANING	EXAMPLES
1. Arch-		A.
		B.
2. Intra-		A.
		B.
3. Contra-		A.
		B.
4. Dia-		A.
		B.
5. Trans-		A.
		B.
6. Post-		A.
		B.
7. Ambi-		A.
		B.
8. Circum-		A.
		B.
9. De-		A.
		B.
10. Inter-		A.
		B.

©Jantzi Test Prep, Inc.
4actprep.com

NOTES

©Jantzi Test Prep, Inc.
4actprep.com

DECODING WORKSHEET III:

IT SUFFIXES TO SAY

DIRECTIONS: Try to define as many of these as you can by yourself by thinking of as many words as you can that end with the suffix you're working on. Then ask yourself, "What do they all have in common?" This should give you the definition.

SUFFIX	MEANING	EXAMPLES
1. -able, -ible		A.
		B.
2. -acious, -ant, -ent, -icious, -ous		A.
		B.
3. —ate		A.
		B.
4. —ation		A.
		B.
5. —cy		A.
		B.
6. —ism		A.
		B.
7. —ist		A.
		B.
8. —ise, -ize		A.
		B.
9. —osis		A.
		B.
10. —tude		A.
		B.

©Jantzi Test Prep, Inc.
4actprep.com

NOTES

©Jantzi Test Prep, Inc.
4actprep.com

ROOTS PRACTICE

DIRECTIONS: In the fourth column of the table, below please write a word that uses the root word to the left. Then, in the fifth column, provide a definition of that word.

Root	Meaning	Example		
a	not	amoral		
ab	away	abrogate		
able	capable of	portable		
acious	full of	audacious		
acr	sharp	acrimonious		
acro	high	acrobat		
act	do	retroactive		
ad	to	adhesive		
agog	leader	demagogue		
agri	field	agriculture		
ali	another	alias		
alter	other	alternator		
amat	love	amatory		
ambi	both	ambidextrous		
ambul	walk	ambulatory		
amor	love	amorous		
amphi	both	amphibious		
an	not, without	anorexic		
andro	man	android		
anim	mind	equanimity		
ann	year	annual		
ant	an agent	fragrant		
ante	before	antedate		
anthrop	man	anthropology		
anti	against	anti-aircraft		

©Jantzi Test Prep, Inc.
4actprep.com

NOTES

©Jantzi Test Prep, Inc.
4actprep.com

anthro	man	anthropology		
apt	fit	adapt		
aqua	water	aquarium		
ar	relating to	pulsar		
arch	chief, rule	monarch		
archy	government	monarchy		
ard	always	drunkard		
ary	like	dictionary		
arthr	joint	arthritis		
astr,aster	star	astronomy		
ation	action, state	irritation		
audi	hear	audience		
auto	self	autobiography		
bas	low	abase		
bell	war	bellow		
bene	good	benefit		
bi	two	bilateral		
biblio	book	bibliography		
bio	life	biography		
brev	short	brevity		
caco	bad	cacophony		
cad	fall	cascade		
cap	take	capture		
cede	go	recede		
cent	one hundred	century		
centri	center	centrifugal		
chron	time	chronometer		

©Jantzi Test Prep, Inc.
4actprep.com

NOTES

©Jantzi Test Prep, Inc.
4actprep.com

ROOTS PRACTICE (CONT'D)

cide	kill	herbicide		
circum	around	circumspect		
cise	cut	circumcise		
cid, cide	kill	homicide		
cit	call	excite		
civi	citizen	civilization		
clam	cry out	clamorous		
cle	small	molecule		
clud	close	exclude		
co	together	cooperate		
cogn	know	recognize		
com	together	combination		
comp	fill	complete		
con	together	contract		
contra	against	contradict		
card, cord	heart	accord		
corp	body	corpulent		
cracy	government	democracy		
cred	believe	credit		
cryo	frozen	cryogenic		
crypt	hidden	cryptic		
culp	blame	culprit		
cur	care for	cure		
curr	run	current		
cy	state of being	democracy		
de	down	deposit		
deb	owe	debt		

©Jantzi Test Prep, Inc.
4actprep.com

NOTES

©Jantzi Test Prep, Inc.
4actprep.com

ROOTS PRACTICE (CONT'D)

dec	ten	decade		
demi	half	demigod		
demo	people	democracy		
derm	skin	dermatologist		
di	day	diary		
dia	across	diagonal		
dicho	two	dichotomy		
dict	say	dictionary		
dign	worthy	dignify		
dis	away	distract		
doc	teach	doctrine		
dom	rule	domination		
dorm	sleep	dormitory		
dox	opinion	orthodox		
duct	lead	conduct		
dyna	power	dynamic		
dys	bad	dysfunctional		
ecto	outer	ectoderm		
ectomy	cut	hysterectomy		
ego	I	egomaniac		
emia	blood	hypoglycemia		
endo	within	endoplasm		
epi	upon	epidermis		
epi	on	epigraph		
equi	equal	equitable		
erg	work	energy		
err	wander	erratic		
ess	female	princess		
eu	good	euphony		

©Jantzi Test Prep, Inc.
4actprep.com

NOTES

©Jantzi Test Prep, Inc.
4actprep.com

ev	age	primeval		
ex	out	exit		
extra	beyond	extraterrestrial		
fac,fact	make	factory		
fall	deceive	fallacious		
fer	carry	transfer		
fic	making	terrific		
fid	faith	infidel		
fin	end	final		
form	shape	conform		
fort	strong	fortitude		
fract	break	fracture		
frat	brother	fraternal		
fug	flee	refugee		
fus	pour	transfusion		
fy	make	fortify		
gamy	marriage	monogamy		
gen	class	gender		
geo	earth	geography		
germ	vital or related	germane		
gest	carry	gestation		
gram	write	telegram		
graph	write	bibliography		
grat	pleasing	gratifying		
greg	group	gregarious		
gyn	women	gynecologist		
gyro	turn	gyration		
hedron	sided object	polyhedron		

©Jantzi Test Prep, Inc.
4actprep.com

NOTES

©Jantzi Test Prep, Inc.
4actprep.com

helio	sun	perihelion		
hema	blood	hematic		
hetero	different	heterodox		
hexa	six	hexagram		
homo	same	homonym		
hydro	water	hydroplane		
hypo	under	hypodermic		
hyper	over	hyperactive		
ician	specialist	technician		
il, ir, im	not	illegal		
in,	in or not	inscribe		
ine	nature of	canine		
inter	between	international		
intra	within	intracellular		
intro	into	introduce		
ism	doctrine	capitalism		
iso	equal	isosceles		
ist	person	fascist		
it	journey	itinerary		
itis	inflammation	arthritis		
ity	state of being	annuity		
ive	like	expensive		
ize	make	victimize		
ject	throw	eject		
junct	join	junction		
jur	swear	jury		
labor	work	laborious		

©Jantzi Test Prep, Inc.
4actprep.com

NOTES

©Jantzi Test Prep, Inc.
4actprep.com

lat	side	bilateral		
leg	read	legible		
lib	book	library		
liber	free	liberate		
lith	rock	neolithic		
loco	place	locomotive		
logy	science	biology		
logy	word	logical		
loqu	talk	soliloquy		
luc	light	lucid		
luna	moon	lunar		
magn	great	magnanimous		
mal	bad	malevolent		
man	hand	manual		
mar	sea	marine		
matri	mother	matricide		
medi	middle	median		
mega	large	megalith		
meso	middle	mesomorph		
meta	change	metamorphosis		
meter	measure	thermometer		
micro	small	micron		
migr	wander	migrate		
milli	thousandth	millipede		
mir	wonder	miracle		
mis	bad	misfit		
miss	send	dismiss		

©Jantzi Test Prep, Inc.
4actprep.com

NOTES

©Jantzi Test Prep, Inc.
4actprep.com

moll	soft	mollify		
mono	one	monotone		
mon	warn	admonish		
morph	shape	amorphous		
mort	death	mortality		
munis	money	remunerate		
muta	change	mutability		
narco	sleep	narcolepsy		
nav	ship	navigate		
nec	kill	internecine		
necro	death	necropolis		
neo	new	neolithic		
nepo	nephew	nepotism		
ness	quality	loch ness		
neuro	nerve	neuron		
nihil	nothing	nihilistic		
nomy	law	astronomy		
non	not	nonstop		
nov	new	novel		
numer	number	enumerate		
nym	name	homonym		
ob	against	obtuse		
obit	death	obituary		
octa	eight	octameter		
ocul	eye	binocular		
oid	appearance	android		

©Jantzi Test Prep, Inc.
4actprep.com

NOTES

104
©Jantzi Test Prep, Inc.
4actprep.com

omni	all	omnivorous		
oper	work	operate		
opia	sight	myopia		
ornith	bird	ornithology		
ortho	straight	orthodox		
osis	condition	psychosis		
osteo	bone	osteopath		
ous	full of	luminous		
pac	peace	pacify		
pan	all	panorama		
par	equal	parity		
para	beside	parable		
pater	father	paternalistic		
path	felling	sympathy		
ped	foot	pedestrian		
ped	teach	pedantic		
pel	drive	repel		
pend	hang	pending		
penta	five	pentagram		
per	through	perception		
pet	seek	petition		
petr	rock	petrify		
phil	love	philanthropy		
phile	love	audiophile		
phobia	fear	claustrophobia		
phon	sound	symphony		
photo	light	photograph		
phys	motion	physiology		

©Jantzi Test Prep, Inc.
4actprep.com

NOTES

©Jantzi Test Prep, Inc.
4actprep.com

plasto	molded	plastic		
platy	flat	plateau		
plu	more	plural		
pluto	wealth	plutocracy		
pod	foot	podiatrist		
polis	city	metropolis		
poly	many	polyphony		
pon	place	postpone		
pond	weight	ponderous		
pop	people	popular		
port	carry	transport		
post	after	postgraduate		
potent	power	omnipotent		
pre	before	prelude		
prim	first	prime		
pro	forward	proliferate		
proto	first	proton		
pseudo	false	pseudonym		
psych	soul	metempsychosis		
pugn	fight	pugnacious		
punct	point, dot	punctuate		
put	think	reputation		
pyro	fire	pyre		
quer	ask	inquiry		
re	again	return		
rect	right	correct		
retro	backward	retroactive		
rid	laugh	ridicule		

©Jantzi Test Prep, Inc.
4actprep.com

NOTES

©Jantzi Test Prep, Inc.
4actprep.com

rog	ask	interrogate		
rupt	break	erupt		
sanct	holy	sanctity		
sangui	blood	sanguinary		
sci	know	science		
scope	look	telescope		
scrib	write	scribble		
se	apart	secede		
sect	cut	dissect		
sed, sid, sess	sit	sediment		
semi	half	semitone		
sens	feel	sense		
sequi	follow	sequence		
solv	loosen	absolve		
som	body	soma		
somn	sleep	somnambulist		
son	sound	sonar		
soph	wisdom	sophomore		
spec	look	spectacles		
spir	breathe	inspire		
stell	star	interstellar		
stereo	solid	stereoscope		
string	bind	stringent		
sub	under	subtract		
super	over	supervise		
sur	over	surplus		
sym	together	sympathy		
syn	together	synthetic		
tact	touch	tactile		

©Jantzi Test Prep, Inc.
4actprep.com

NOTES

©Jantzi Test Prep, Inc.
4actprep.com

tang	touch	tangible		
tele	distance	telephone		
tempor	time	temporal		
ten	hold	tenure		
terr	land	terrestrial		
tetra	four	tetrameter		
theo	god	theology		
thermo	heat	thermostat		
tion	act or state	completion		
topo	place	topographical		
tort	twist	contorted		
tract	pull	tractor		
trans	across	transfer		
tri	three	tricycle		
trib	pay	tribute		
troph	growth	hypertrophy		
ultra	beyond	ultramarine		
un	not	unfit		
uni	one	unicorn		
urb	city	urban		
veni	come	intervene		
ver	true	verify		
vest	clothes	vestibule		
via	way	trivial		
vid	look	video		
vita	life	vitamin		
viv	life	vivid		

©Jantzi Test Prep, Inc.
4actprep.com

NOTES

©Jantzi Test Prep, Inc.
4actprep.com

MATH

STRATEGIES

©Jantzi Test Prep, Inc.
4actprep.com

NOTES

©Jantzi Test Prep, Inc.
4actprep.com

THE SUBSTITUTE PRINCIPLE

1. Many types of ACT math problems not necessarily focus on testing your math skills. The test makers try to write problems which can be solved using reasoning skills. This means that sometimes methods other than the ones you use in math class are needed on the test. One such method is "The Substitute Principle."

2. "The Substitute Principle," which may be used on all types of math problems listed above, simply says, that when possible, you should substitute numbers for variables.

3. There are three types of numbers that you can substitute for variables:
   their numbers (answer choices), your numbers and "magic numbers"

4. On all multiple-choice problems that ask for the value of a variable, you can either substitute an answer choice or your own number for the variable. On student-produced response questions, you must substitute your own number.

5. When substituting your own numbers, use the magic numbers $(2, 1, 0, -2, \frac{1}{2})$ whenever possible since they represent all of the different types of numbers (positive, negative, fractions). For some problems involving time, mph, or percent, use 60, -60, and 100 respectively.

6. If there are two or more variables, make sure that your substitution makes the statement true.

7. If the problem is very difficult, you may get stuck. Remember, though, that you may be far enough along in the problem to eliminate some wrong answer choices and therefore guess.

Sample problem: If $0 < x < 1$, which of the following statements must be true?

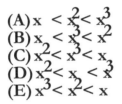

(A) $x < x^2 < x^3$
(B) $x_2 < x^3 < x^2$
(C) $x^2 < x^3 < x_3$
(D) $x^2 < x_3 < x^3$
(E) $x^3 < x^2 < x$

©Jantzi Test Prep, Inc.
4actprep.com

NOTES

©Jantzi Test Prep, Inc.
4actprep.com

BD IS YOUR BUDDY!

1. Most answer choices to regular math questions on the SAT are in order from the smallest value to the largest value or vice versa. This means "**A**" and "**E**" will always be the smallest or biggest value. For example:

| (A) 3 | (B) 6 | (C) 8 | (D) 10 | (E) 11 |

OR

| (A) 11 | (B) 10 | (C) 8 | (D) 6 | (E) 3 |

2. If the question asks for the value of a variable like "x", "y" or "n", always plug in choice "**B**" first because you then know that:

When the choices are ordered from small to big (**A-E**):

- If the value you plug in for "**B**" works out perfectly, "**B**" is the answer.

- If the value you plug in for "**B**" is too large, your answer is "**A**."

- If the value you plug in for "**B**" is too small, you quickly eliminate "**A**" and "**B**". You then plug in "**D**." "**D**" may be the answer, but if "**D**" is too large, then the answer is "**C**"; if "**D**" is too small, then the answer is "**E**."

When the choices are ordered from big to small (**E-A**):

- If the value you plug in for "**B**" works out perfectly, "**B**" is the answer.

- If the value you plug in for "**B**" is too small, your answer is "**A**."

- If the value you plug in for "**B**" is too large, you quickly eliminate "**A**" and "**B**." You then plug in "**D**." "**D**" may be the answer, but if "**D**" is too small, then the answer is "**C**"; if "**D**" is too large, then the answer is "**E**."

Sample Problems:

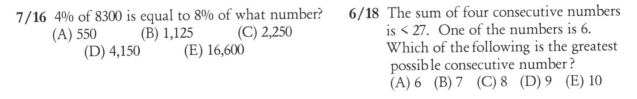

7/16 4% of 8300 is equal to 8% of what number?
    (A) 550   (B) 1,125   (C) 2,250
       (D) 4,150   (E) 16,600

6/18 The sum of four consecutive numbers is < 27. One of the numbers is 6. Which of the following is the greatest possible consecutive number?
(A) 6 (B) 7 (C) 8 (D) 9 (E) 10

©Jantzi Test Prep, Inc.
4actprep.com

NOTES

©Jantzi Test Prep, Inc.
4actprep.com

THE ROMAN CONQUEST (circa 2010 A.D.)

If you encounter a math problem that's Greek to you, it's actually a Roman numeral problem. These problems look like this:

4/8 If $w < x < z$ and $w < y < z$, which of the following statements must be true?

I. $w < z$
II. $x < y$
III. $y < z$

(A) I only
(B) II only
(C) III only
(D) I and III only
(E) I, II, and III

14/16 If $3x = \dfrac{1}{2}y + 1$, which of the following statements must be true?

I.   x and y must be even integers.
II. x and y must be consecutive integers.
III. x and y must be integers.

(A) None
(B) II only
(C) I and III
(D) II and III
(E) III only

Use the following steps to "conquer" these problems:

1. Try to solve the equation in terms of one of the variables.

2. Using the Substitute Principle, plug in your own easy numbers for the variables so that it makes the given statement true. Remember, you can also use the magic numbers 2, 1, 0, -2, $\dfrac{1}{2}$ to make sure that you cover the possibilities created by all types of numbers.

3. You don't have to deal with the Roman numerals in the order they are presented. If you can quickly and easily determine if II or III is true or false, then deal with these Roman numerals first.

4. Even if you can only determine that one of the Roman numerals is false, this will usually allow you to eliminate a couple of answers.

5. If you can eliminate even one of the answer choices, you must guess.

©Jantzi Test Prep, Inc.
4actprep.com

NOTES

©Jantzi Test Prep, Inc.
4actprep.com

A PICTURE IS WORTH A THOUSAND WORDS

Follow these simple rules whenever the problem requires a diagram that is or isn't illustrated.

1a. If a diagram is provided: Determine if the figure is drawn to scale (DTS). Most diagrams are drawn to scale, which means that the drawing's proportions and measurements are exactly as they appear. In other words, if one side of a figure that is drawn to scale looks longer than another side, it *is* longer, and the measurements could be proven mathematically or by use of a ruler. Here's how you determine if a figure is drawn to scale:

> ➤ When a figure is not drawn to scale (NFNDTS) the diagram will have a disclaimer beneath it that says so: "NOTE: *Figure is not drawn to scale.*" However, you <u>can trust</u> what is given to you; for example, if they tell you an angle measures 90°, then it measures 90°. You just can't assume any information that isn't given. If the figure is not drawn to scale you can either take the drawing with a "grain of salt" or quickly re-draw the diagram.

> ➤ If the figure is drawn to scale (DTS), no disclaimer will appear and you can trust your eyes.

1b. If a diagram is not provided:

> ➤ Then you must quickly decide if you need to draw your own (DYO).

2. The next step is to make sure all pertinent information is labeled on the figure. Many times the test-makers do not put all the information on the diagram because <u>it would make the problem too easy</u>. Therefore, transfer all given information, as well as any information that you can easily determine based on the given information, onto the drawing.

3. Now look for some perspective. Find something that is known on the diagram to which you can compare the unknown. If you already know the area or perimeter of an object, you should then compare the unknown to the known perimeter or area in order to determine the approximate measurements of the unknown.

4. Next, don't be afraid to draw on the figure. You paid the money, so it's your booklet. Sketch on the diagram if it helps you simplify the problem. Don't be afraid to cut and paste mentally by moving something on a diagram to a location where it simplifies the drawing. Also, sometimes the answer is easier to see if the diagram is rotated a $\frac{1}{4}$, $\frac{1}{2}$ or $\frac{3}{4}$ turn.

5. Remember you can always use the ruler or protractor strategies you learned in the course on (DTS) problems.

©Jantzi Test Prep, Inc.
4actprep.com

NOTES

©Jantzi Test Prep, Inc.
4actprep.com

A PICTURE IS WORTH A THOUSAND WORDS (CONT'D)

DTS Problem

7/16 Which value is closest to the area of the shaded region if the area of the largest circle is 36π?

(A) 3π
(B) 6π
(C) 9π
(D) 12π
(E) 15π

FNDTS Problem

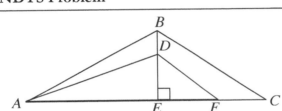

Note: Figure not drawn to scale.

14/18 In $\triangle ABC$ above, $\dfrac{BD}{BE}\,\Delta\,\dfrac{1}{4}$ and $\dfrac{AF}{AC}\,\Delta\,\dfrac{6}{9}$.

What is the value of $\dfrac{\text{area } \triangle ADF}{\text{area } \triangle ABC}$?

DYO Problem

12/18 Two sides of an isosceles triangle have lengths of 20 and 35. What is the greatest possible value of the triangle's perimeter?

©Jantzi Test Prep, Inc.
4actprep.com

NOTES

©Jantzi Test Prep, Inc.
4actprep.com

OPTICAL DELUSIONS

5

1. What geometric figure(s) do you see? _____

2. How many of each? _____ , _____

3. How many did Bobby see? _____

4. Is the diagram drawn to scale? _____

5. If so, what can you assume about the identity of the smaller figures?_____

6. What is the perimeter and area of the smallest figure? P =_____ , A =_____

7. What is the perimeter and area of the largest figure?   P =_____ , A =_____

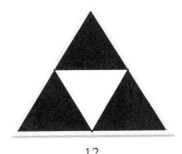

12

1. How many triangles do you see? _____

2. How many did Bobby see? _____

3. Is the diagram drawn to scale? _____

4. If so, what can you assume about the triangles?

5. What is the perimeter and area of a small triangle? P =_____ , A =_____

©Jantzi Test Prep, Inc.
4actprep.com

NOTES

©Jantzi Test Prep, Inc.
4actprep.com

SPRLATIVES/GRID-INS

1. **You don't have to answer all the questions.** This is especially true here. Unless you have a 600+ math score you should *not* try to answer all of them. If you only answer 8 out of 10, and if you try hard to get all of them right, this will more than make up for not attempting all of them. You should still bubble in an answer to every question even though it's a wild guess. This is the only type of question where there is no penalty at all for incorrect answers.

2. **These types of questions are open-ended** and therefore take more time than regular multiple-choice type math problems. Make sure you adjust for this.

3. **Because you don't have any answer choices to look at,** you will not have anything to gauge how close you are to the right answer. So it's very important not to make stupid mistakes here because you will not have a safety net.

4. **If there is no diagram, draw one.**

5. **If you don't know what to do, don't guess an answer – guess how to work the problem.** Since you have a very small chance of guessing the right answer, the best option you have is to guess how to work the problem. You may just get it right, or you may figure out how to work the problem. The key here is to just try something – do not leave it blank.

6. **Make sure you understand the directions for bubbling Grid-Ins.**

   A. Write the answers in the boxes first, and then bubble in the ovals.

   B. If you come up with a negative number for an answer, it's wrong.

   C. Mark only one oval per column.

   D. Always slam your answer all the way to the right.

   E. Don't round off your answers. The answer should always be in the most accurate form. For example, if your calculator reads .333…, .33 is wrong. You should put .333.

   F. Do not grid-in mixed numbers. Convert them to improper fractions or decimals first.

   $$3\frac{1}{2} = \frac{7}{2}$$

©Jantzi Test Prep, Inc.
4actprep.com

NOTES

©Jantzi Test Prep, Inc.
4actprep.com

BIG ANGLE/SMALL ANGLE

This strategy works when you have one or more pair(s) of parallel lines and a transversal(s).

1. If a pair of lines appears to be parallel, such as those in the diagrams below, you can just extend the lines. This helps tremendously to see the parallel lines easier.

A    B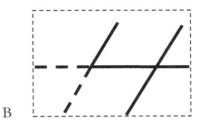

2. Even though the diagram has eight angles, there are only two different sizes of angles: **big** and **small**.

3. There will always be some given information to start the problem. Make sure all information is labeled on the diagram. (see *A Picture's Worth a Thousand Words*).

4. If an angle is given to be, or can be determined to be, less than 90°, all angles that look less than 90° are the same size angle. Likewise, all angles that look greater than 90°are the same size angles.

5. Now you use the Diffusion Principle. Start from the area of the highest concentration of information and work towards the area of the lowest concentration of information (what they are asking you to solve).

6. The most important thing here is the vertical angles concept. They will never use the term "vertical angles," but you have to know how to use the concept.

©Jantzi Test Prep, Inc.
4actprep.com

NOTES

©Jantzi Test Prep, Inc.
4actprep.com

BIG ANGLE/ SMALL ANGLE (CONT'D)

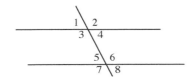

2/8 If a given line intersects two parallel lines, then the sum of the measures of angles 2 and 3 must equal the sum of the angles of which pair?

    (A) 5 and 6
    (B) 5 and 8
    (C) 6 and 8
    (D) 6 and 7
    (E) 7 and 8

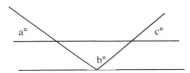

Note: Figure not drawn to scale

3/16 Given the diagram above, the 2 horizontal lines are parallel. If $a = 60$ and $c = 50$, what is the value of b?

    (A) 50
    (B) 60
    (C) 70
    (D) 90
    (E) 110

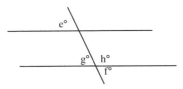

Note: Figure not drawn to scale

6/16 Given the diagram above, the 2 horizontal lines are parallel and $e = 70$. What is the value of $f + g - h$?

    (A) 20
    (B) 30
    (C) 40
    (D) 50
    (E) 60

©Jantzi Test Prep, Inc.
4actprep.com

NOTES

©Jantzi Test Prep, Inc.
4actprep.com

PIZZA TIME!

This strategy will help you on problems that resemble a clock or a pizza.

Any time a problem discusses or has a diagram with a round figure, it's Pizza Time! The best way to figure out the area of a circle is to relate it to a pizza or a clock. What they are really asking is if you know there are 360 degrees around a circle.

12.18 Each piece of the pizza you ordered has a tip touching the center of the whole pizza. The angle at the tip (central angle) is always greater than 30° and less than 35°. What is the maximum number of slices of pizza?

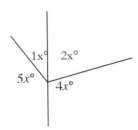

6.16 In the figure above, four line segments meet at a point to form four angles. What is the value of x?

©Jantzi Test Prep, Inc.
4actprep.com

NOTES

©Jantzi Test Prep, Inc.
4actprep.com

PIZZA TIME! (CONT'D)

Have you ever wondered if getting a bigger pizza is worth 2-4 dollars more? If so, take a look at this.

Say you're trying to decide if getting the 12-inch personal pan pizza instead of the 10-inch is worth the extra few dollars.

10-inch	r = 5	$A = \pi r^2$	$A = \pi(5)^2$	$A = 78.5$ in^2
12-inch	r = 6	$A = \pi r^2$	$A = \pi(6)^2$	$A = 113.04$ in^2
14-inch	r = 7	$A = \pi r^2$	$A = \pi(7)^2$	$A = 153.86$ in^2
16-inch	r = 8	$A = \pi r^2$	$A = \pi(8)^2$	$A = 200.76$ in^2
18-inch	r = 9	$A = \pi r^2$	$A = \pi(9)^2$	$A = 254.34$ in^2

Because of exponents, a small increase in radius makes a big difference in how much hot and delicious pizza you get. Keep this in mind when comparing a small circle inside a large one. For example, a 14-inch pizza has almost twice as much deliciousness as a 10-inch pie.

©Jantzi Test Prep, Inc.
4actprep.com

NOTES

©Jantzi Test Prep, Inc.
4actprep.com

VICIOUS CIRCLES

1. The best formula for circumference is πD. 2πr is too similar to πr², the formula for area. If they give you radius, double it, and that's the diameter.

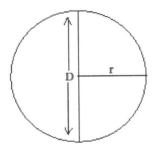

2. Circumference is just a fancy name for the perimeter of a circle.
3. Remember, if it has a diagram, check to see if it's drawn to scale. If there is no diagram, draw one. (*A Picture's Worth A Thousand Words*)
4. Again, are they asking for: outside (circumference) or inside (area)?

16/18 If the perplexed alien pictured above has eyes with radius 2, what is the area of his sunburned forehead (shaded region)?
A) 16 π B) 8 π C) 6 π
D) 4 π E) 2 π

18/20 What is the perimeter of the shaded region?
A) 16 π B) 8 π C) 6 π
D) 4 π E) 2 π

©Jantzi Test Prep, Inc.
4actprep.com

NOTES

©Jantzi Test Prep, Inc.
4actprep.com

ANSWER "DUH" QUESTION

1. The first thing you do to any math problem that consists mostly of words is read it carefully to get a good understanding of what they are asking for.

2. If there is a figure or diagram, take the information from the problem and label it on the drawing.

3. The SAT is notorious for asking for x + 5. In other words, after you have solved for x (the variable) they ask you to add 5 to it. When this is the case, circle what they are asking for. You can bet if they want you to solve for x + 5, the answer choices will include the value of x as well to trick those students who forget to add 5 to their answer!

4. Believe it or not, many students read a question that asks you to solve for perimeter and then they solve for area instead. You'd better believe that the answer for area will be among the choices! The words that tend to be confusing are integers, consecutive odd, even etc. and remainder. They also often ask for the average and then include the words "arithmetic mean" right after it. This is there to get you to second-guess yourself.

5. Remember, they always have to provide everything you need to solve the problem. Therefore you should start with the given information and develop a general plan.

6. The last important thing to remember about word problems is to try to rephrase the questions if you can, in simpler terms. Ask yourself, "What are they really saying here?"

FIGURES AND DIAGRAMS

There are four questions that you have to ask yourself when working with figures and diagrams.

1. What type of figure am I working with?
2. What formulas apply to this specific type of diagram?
3. What rules or principles do I know about this diagram?
4. What are they looking for?

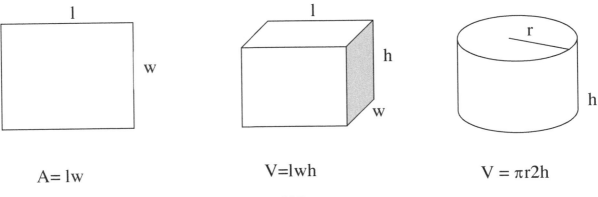

$A = lw$ $\qquad\qquad$ $V = lwh$ $\qquad\qquad$ $V = \pi r2h$

©Jantzi Test Prep, Inc.
4actprep.com

NOTES

©Jantzi Test Prep, Inc.
4actprep.com

THE DIFFUSION PRINCIPLE

Diffusion is the movement from an area of higher concentration to an area of lower concentration.

1. This is a global concept that should be used on all math problems.

2. The biggest mistake(s) a student can make on the SAT math section is either:

   ➤ Not knowing where to start when solving a math problem, and/or

   ➤ Solving for things that are not needed to arrive at the right answer.

3. The Diffusion Principle simply stated is: work from the area of highest concentration of information to the area of lowest concentration of information in order to find the answer. This is similar to working backwards.

4. When you decide to go on a vacation, what is the first decision you make? Answer: Where you are going to go. Once you know that, every subsequent decision is based on where you are going. Now you must figure out HOW you will get there. Plane, train, automobile, etc. Then you decide what route to take. On a diagram problem, work from where the given information is toward the unknown. Just like taking a trip, you want to go the most direct route. This will alleviate solving for unnecessary information.

5. When you are working on a word problem you have to do something with the given information.

   ➤ First decide if anything given is unnecessary.

   ➤ Then decide how you are going to use what is given in light of the diffusion principal.

6. Remember, the shortest path between two points is a straight line. Therefore try to work directly to the unknown (even though that is not always possible.)

©Jantzi Test Prep, Inc.
4actprep.com

NOTES

©Jantzi Test Prep, Inc.
4actprep.com

CALCULATOR USE

1. **Use a calculator that you are comfortable with.** It is ridiculous to think you will use a graphing calculator for the exam if you've never used it before. You're better off with a six function "el cheapo" if that's the one you're used to.

2. **Bring a back-up calculator.** You don't want your battery to run out in the middle of the SAT. You can bring a spare battery, but remember that putting in the spare could waste valuable time on the test while a spare calculator could be used right away.

3. **Leave the power on at all times during the test. Take it out of the jacket if it has one.** That way you don't have to hold back the cover while you're pushing the buttons. It might not be a bad idea to have some tape and tape it down to the corner of your desk during the exam. This would enable you to use one hand to punch the buttons while the other hand is free to write.

4. **Just because you are using a calculator doesn't guarantee every answer is correct.** Don't forget to engage your brain while you're copying the information from the calculator's display. Ask yourself, "Does this look right?" and "Is this what I expected?" If not, you should check your answers. Two simple calculation errors can cost you 20 points on the SAT, so not checking your work could be the equivalent of throwing away 20 points on the test.

5. **Don't bring the following calculators** because they are not allowed: Calculators with: typewriter key pad, paper tape for printout, or AC cord for power. Laptops or mini computers and pocket organizers are also illegal.

6. **Don't try to share** a calculator with a friend – that's illegal too!

7. **Always look for short cuts.** Don't get tricked into doing long, tedious operations on your calculator. This is a trap.

©Jantzi Test Prep, Inc.
4actprep.com

NOTES

©Jantzi Test Prep, Inc.
4actprep.com

FRATIOS

Fractions are ratios. Ratios are just fractions that are vertically challenged.

1. There are a few things that are assumed to be true about any number; see example below:

   7 is really

   ➢ All numbers are positive unless stated otherwise.

   ➢ All numbers are to the 1st power unless stated otherwise.

   ➢ All numbers have 1 as a denominator unless otherwise stated.
   In other words **all numbers** are…fractions!

2. Fractions are numbers that are used for two reasons. Sometimes the test-makers just use them to mess with your head, and sometimes they're used when the value isn't a whole number. For example, $\frac{4}{2}$ could be reduced to 2. But $\frac{5}{2}$ could not be reduced to a whole number, so it has to be expressed as a fraction.

3. When fractions are expressed as ratios, you trade in the "surfboard" ($\frac{3}{2}$) for a colon (3:2). Remember, colons always stink!

4. A fraction simply asks you how many times the bottom number divides into the top number. So in other words, a fraction is just a division problem!

   Sample Problems:

1/8   If $y + \frac{3}{y} = 7 + \frac{3}{7}$, then y can equal:

   (A) 0

   (B) $\frac{1}{3}$

   (C) 1

   (D) 3

   (E) 7

©Jantzi Test Prep, Inc.
4actprep.com

NOTES

©Jantzi Test Prep, Inc.
4actprep.com

FRATIOS (CONT'D)

11/20 If b is directly proportional to a, and if b = 12 when a = 5, what is the value of b when a = 7.5?

(A) $\frac{5}{18}$

(B) $\frac{5}{12}$

(C) 12

(D) 16

(E) 18

15/20 Red, yellow, and orange paint are combined in the ratio 2:2:1, respectively, to create a certain new color of paint. To make 10 gallons of this new color, how many gallons of yellow paint are required?

(A) $\frac{2}{5}$

(B) 1

(C) 2

(D) 4

(E) 5

10/16 A toy chest contains only black, brown and green blocks. The probability of randomly selecting a black block is $\frac{1}{3}$, and the probability of randomly selecting a brown block is $\frac{1}{5}$. Which of the following could be the total number of blocks in the toy chest?

(A) 18

(B) 20

(C) 25

(D) 30

(E) 35

16/18 A malicious tot mixed a near-lethal beverage and dared other kids to drink it. He started with $\frac{1}{4}$ a cup of milk in an 8 oz. glass. He then added equal amounts of tomato juice, prune juice, milk, and olive oil. Yuck! What fraction of the final concoction was milk?

©Jantzi Test Prep, Inc.
4actprep.com

NOTES

©Jantzi Test Prep, Inc.
4actprep.com

WE'RE GIVING YOU THE THIRD DEGREE

Every thing you ever wanted to know about the degree measures inside a triangle.

1. There are only two things to solve for in a triangle on the SAT:

    ➤ The length of the sides or

    ➤ The measure of an angle(s) inside the triangle.

2. Students often confuse the two because they are interdependent.

3. The Third Degree deals with anything <u>inside</u> a triangle, not perimeter. This includes the Pythagorean Theorem, the sum of angles, bisectors, right angles, etc.

4. The first thing you have to know is that there are always 180 degrees inside a triangle. They will beat this to death on the SAT.

5. The Pythagorean theorem $(a^2 + b^2 = c^2)$ only works on right triangles.

6. The longest side of a triangle is always across from the largest angle. A hypotenuse is a special name for the longest side of a right triangle. If a triangle doesn't contain a right angle, even if there is a big angle, there could be another angle just as large. For example, an 80, 80, 20.

7. There is a direct relationship between the size of an angle and the side opposite from it. The larger an angle, the larger proportionately is the opposite side, and vise-versa

Sample Problems:

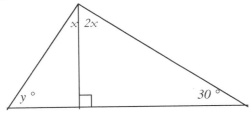

7/20 In the figure above, what is the value of angle y ?
    (A) 45
    (B) 50
    (C) 55
    (D) 60
    (E) 80

11/18 Three angles in a triangle measure x, $3x$, and y, where x is greater than 40°. If x and y are integers, what is one possible value of y ?

©Jantzi Test Prep, Inc.
4actprep.com

NOTES

©Jantzi Test Prep, Inc.
4actprep.com

WE'RE GIVING YOU THE THIRD DEGREE (CONT'D)

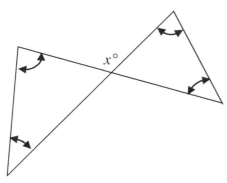

15/16 In the figure above, what is the sum, in terms of x, of the degree measures of the four marked angles?

(A) x
(B) 2x
(C) 3x
(D) 180 − x
(E) 360 − x

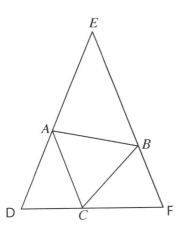

19/20 In the diagram above, isosceles triangle DEF contains equilateral triangle ABC inscribed inside. The measure of $\angle DEF$ is 40° and $\angle EBA$ is 55°. What is the measure of $\angle ACD$?

(A) 60
(B) 65
(C) 70
(D) 75
(E) 80

©Jantzi Test Prep, Inc.
4actprep.com

NOTES

©Jantzi Test Prep, Inc.
4actprep.com

WE'RE GIVING YOU THE THIRD DEGREE (CONT'D)

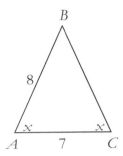 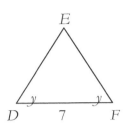

15/20 If $y = 60$ in $\triangle DEF$ above, how much greater is the perimeter of $\triangle ABC$ than the perimeter of $\triangle DEF$?

(A) 2
(B) 3
(C) 4
(D) 5
(E) 6

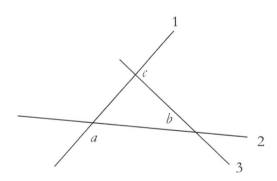

Note: Figure not drawn to scale.

13/16 In the figure above, if $b = 25$, what is the value of $a + c$?

(A) 155
(B) 180
(C) 205
(D) 270
(E) 360

©Jantzi Test Prep, Inc.
4actprep.com

NOTES

©Jantzi Test Prep, Inc.
4actprep.com

WE'RE GIVING YOU THE THIRD DEGREE (CONT'D)

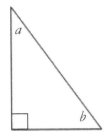 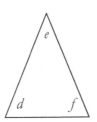

6/16 What is the average (arithmetic mean) of *a*, *b*, *d*, *e*, and *f* ?

(A) 30
(B) 45
(C) 50
(D) 54
(E) 60

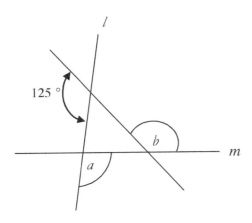

17/20 In the figure above, $a + b = $?

(A) 120
(B) 180
(C) 210
(D) 235
(E) 250

©Jantzi Test Prep, Inc.
4actprep.com

NOTES

©Jantzi Test Prep, Inc.
4actprep.com

PYTHAGOREAN THEOREM

Pythagoras was a really smart Greek philosopher who lived on the island of Samos around 500 B.C. The problem was that he was lonely on that island and had no life. So, he dreamed up the famous theorem that bears his name.

It states: $A^2 + B^2 = C^2$

Remember "We're Giving You the Third Degree?" It dealt with stuff inside a triangle. This page deals with the outside. Now, you still have to pay attention to stuff inside a triangle to do these, because the hypotenuse (C^2) has to be opposite the 90 degree angle (the biggest one).

For those of us with a life, it just means that if you square the largest side (the hypotenuse) of a <u>right</u> triangle (triangle with a 90 degree angle), it will equal the sum of the squares of the other two sides. Here are a few sample problems. Remember, if there's no diagram, draw one!

12/18   How far will a man fall to his death if he falls off the top of a 16-foot ladder leaning against a building if its base is 5 feet from the wall? Round to the nearest foot.

11/18   Billy is a redneck. He is dared by his buddies to swim across a ragin' river 500 yards wide. He begins swimming and miraculously doesn't drown. He ends up 125 yards downstream when he reaches the other side. How far did this idiot swim?

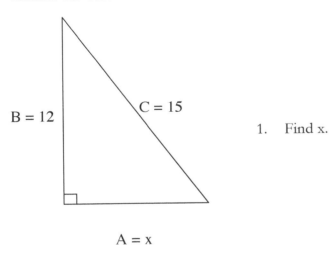

B = 12

C = 15

A = x

1.   Find x.

Did you notice it's a Pythagorean triple?

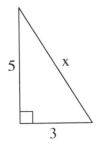

5

x

3

2. Find x.

See – not all triangles with sides of 3 and 5 are Pythagorean triples! (3, 4, 5)

©Jantzi Test Prep, Inc.
4actprep.com

NOTES

©Jantzi Test Prep, Inc.
4actprep.com

YOU ARE 100 PERCENT CORRECT

1. Problems involving percent are simply asking you one thing: what is a certain amount out of a whole? A whole anything is 100 %. Therefore whenever you have the option to substitute for a variable, plug in 100. If the price of an object is the variable, substitute 100.

2. To multiply, think of percents as money.
    $$40\% = .40 = 40 \text{ cents}$$
    $$75\% = .75 = 75 \text{ cents}$$
    $$100\% = 1.00 = 100 \text{ cents}$$

3. See problem #7/16 on the next page.

4. Percent is decimals! It's just code. There are two little circles in a percent sign %. The two little circles are an ancient cue to tell people that they should move the decimal point two places to the left starting from the end of the number. For instance, 80% = 80.0, and therefore = .80 when converted.

5. To increase a number by 10%, multiply by 1.10. This will yield the answer in one step. 1.10 = 1.00 (the original number) + the .10 part. This increases the original number by 10%. To decrease a number by 10%, multiply by .90. This automatically deducts 10% from the original number. This saves time, takes one step out of the process, and reduces your chances of making a dumb mistake.

6. Remember to use the diffusion principle.

Sample Problems:

    4/16   If 0.08 percent of x is 8, what is 8 percent of x?
          (A) .8
          (B) 8
          (C) 80
          (D) 800
          (E) 8000

© Jantzi Test Prep, Inc.
4actprep.com

NOTES

©Jantzi Test Prep, Inc.
4actprep.com

7/16   If 0.008 percent of x is 8, what is x?

(A) 800
(B) 1000
(C) 10,000
(D) 12,222
(E) 18,000

12/20   What is the greatest possible integer for which 40 percent of that integer is less then 6.8?

(A) 9
(B) 10
(C) 14
(D) 17
(E) 18

13/16   The price of a DVD player was first decreased by 15 percent and then increased by 20 percent. What percent of the initial price is the final price?

(A) 98.5%
(B) 100%
(C) 102%
(D) 106.25%
(E) 110%

16/18   If $x + 3y$ is equal to 150 percent of $6y$, what is the value of $\dfrac{y}{x}$?

©Jantzi Test Prep, Inc.
4actprep.com

NOTES

©Jantzi Test Prep, Inc.
4actprep.com

TRICK (OR TREAT?) MATH PROBLEMS

1. *How do you know if it's a trick question?*

    Very simple – they look easy, but the problem number says they are hard! Trick questions are almost always SPRs (no answer choices). You should also notice that most trick questions don't have diagrams.

2. *Why not?*

    Cuz diagrams almost always make the problem easier. That's why we ask you to draw one if one is not provided.

3. *What do I do?*

    You have two options:

    a. You're at the end of the section, so you can obviously omit it, or...

    b. You could answer it, but you really have to be careful to get it right. You've probably got only one minute left in the section, but most of the time, these are SPRs. If you get them wrong, no biggie – you don't lose any points. If it's SPR, you must solve it all the way out because there are no answer choices. If it's RMC and you can get far enough to find a couple wrong answers, you should guess.

Here are a few sample problems. Remember, they are all at the end of math sections.

14/18 Six times a number is the same as the number added to six. What is the number?

15/18 The greatest integer of a set of consecutive numbers is 13. If the sum of the integers is -14, how many integers are in this set?

17/18 What is the product of the least prime number greater than 40 and the greatest prime number less than 40?

©Jantzi Test Prep, Inc.
4actprep.com

NOTES

©Jantzi Test Prep, Inc.
4actprep.com

PERCENTS AND DECIMALS

A decimal is just a fraction.

➢ $0.5 = \dfrac{1}{2}$ Divide the bottom into the top.

Decimals also represent percentages

➢ 0.5 = 50% Multiply decimals by 100 to get a percent. Divide percents by 100 to get a decimal

➢ Decimal two places to right = percent. Percent two places to left = decimal number.

➢ Treat percents like money: 50% is $0.50; 100% is $1.00 or 1 whole.

Changing percents into fractions

➢ Put the number over 100, lose the percent sign and simplify.

➢ $36\% = \dfrac{36}{100} = \dfrac{9}{25}$

Change these percentages to fractions:	Change these decimals to percentages:
• 70% =	• .36 =
• 34% =	• 2.25 =
• 40% =	• .15 =
• 87% =	• .005 =
Change these fractions to percentages:	**Change these percentages to decimals:**
• $\dfrac{1}{2}$ • $\dfrac{6}{33}$	• 24% =
	• 49% =
• $\dfrac{3}{4}$ • $\dfrac{19}{20}$	• 200% =
	• 8% =

©Jantzi Test Prep, Inc.
4actprep.com

NOTES

©Jantzi Test Prep, Inc.
4actprep.com

MATH FUNDAMENTALS

PEMDAS – **P**lease **E**xcuse **M**y **D**ear **A**unt **S**ally

The Order of Operations

Do Parentheses, then Exponents, then Multiplication and Division from left to right, then Addition and Subtraction from Left to Right.

$$\frac{3(5+7)+6\ +\ 3+4}{2}=7$$

Associative Law – Order Doesn't Matter

Addition and Multiplication

When adding and multiplying, the order of the numbers doesn't matter.

$$4+5=5+4\quad\&\quad3+2=2+3$$

Distributive Law – Multiplying Spreads

Parentheses

Multiplication distributes across parentheses.

$$x(y+z)=xy+xz\quad\&\quad3(5+2)=15+6=21$$

Definitions – Things you need to know

Words and Stuff

The **sum** is the answer to an **addition** problem.

The **difference** is the answer to a **subtraction** problem.

The **product** is the answer to a **multiplication** problem.

The **quotient** is the answer to a **division** problem.

Simplify, expand, or factor.	
• $6(57+23)-2\gamma4=$	• $xy(ab+cd-ef)=$
• $2\gamma5^2-\dfrac{21}{7}=$	• $6+2-9\gamma6+3+(5^3-5)=$
• $x(y+z+q)=$	• $3x+3y=$
• $xyz+ayz=$	• $abx-ax+acdx=$

©Jantzi Test Prep, Inc.
4actprep.com

NOTES

©Jantzi Test Prep, Inc.
4actprep.com

EXPONENTS, ROOTS AND RADICALS

Rules

➤ All numbers are potential bases and are automatically to the 1st power.

$$4 = 4^1$$

➤ 1 to any power equals 1.

➤ Any number to the zero power is 1.

➤ Any number to the power of 1 equals that number.

➤ If you square a number between 0 and 1 it gets smaller.

➤ Only terms that look alike can be added, and then the exponents do not change.

$$x^3 + x^3 = 2x^3$$

➤ When multiplying numbers with like bases, add the exponents.

    ○ $2^4 \bullet 2^3 = 2^{4+3} = 2^7$

➤ When dividing numbers with like bases, subtract the exponents.

    ○ $z^8 \div z^6 = z^{8-6} = z^2$

➤ When one power is raised to another, the mistake-free way is to add the exponents.

    ○ $(5^3)^2 = 5^3 \bullet 5^3 = 5^{3+3} = 5^6$

➤ A negative number to an even power is positive.

➤ A negative number to an odd power is negative.

Radical Rules

$$\sqrt{xy} = \sqrt{x} \bullet \sqrt{y} = \sqrt{9} \bullet \sqrt{25} = 3 \bullet 5 = 15$$

$$\sqrt{\frac{x}{y}} = \sqrt{\frac{4}{9}} = \frac{2}{3}$$

©Jantzi Test Prep, Inc.
4actprep.com

NOTES

©Jantzi Test Prep, Inc.
4actprep.com

JANTZI™
✓ TEST PREP

EXPONENTS, ROOTS AND RADICALS (CONT'D)

Practice Problems:

- $\sqrt{\dfrac{9}{16}} =$

- $\sqrt{3} \cdot \sqrt{3} =$

- $\dfrac{\sqrt{4}}{\sqrt{25}} =$

- $\sqrt{40} =$

- $4^3 =$

- $x^3 \cdot x^2 =$

- $(z^3)^2 =$

- $2x^3 + 3x^3 =$

- $y^3 + y^4 =$

- $4^3 \div 4 =$

- $6 \cdot 3^1 =$

- $5^0 =$

- $\sqrt{16} \cdot \sqrt{4} =$

- $\sqrt[3]{27} =$

- $\dfrac{\sqrt{1}}{\sqrt{36}} =$

- $z^3 \cdot z^4 =$

- $\dfrac{8^9}{8^2} =$

- $(x^3)^3 =$

- $x^{-2} =$

- $3^{-3} =$

- $(y^4)^2 =$

©Jantzi Test Prep, Inc.
4actprep.com

NOTES

©Jantzi Test Prep, Inc.
4actprep.com

FRACTIONS ARE FUNKY

Fractions are ratios of whole numbers.

i.e., $\dfrac{1}{2}, \dfrac{1}{4}, \dfrac{3}{4}$

Fractions have two parts
- ➤ The numerator (top) tells how many parts you have.
- ➤ The denominator (bottom) tells how many parts there are in the whole.

Fractions can be added and subtracted.
- ➤ You may need to change the denominators so that they will be the same.

$$\dfrac{1}{2}+\dfrac{3}{4}=\dfrac{2}{4}+\dfrac{3}{4}=\dfrac{5}{4} \qquad\qquad \dfrac{5}{4}-\dfrac{1}{2}=\dfrac{5}{4}-\dfrac{2}{4}=\dfrac{3}{4}$$

Fractions can be multiplied
- ➤ Just multiply the numerators and denominators and simplify.

$$\dfrac{2}{5}\bullet\dfrac{3}{4}=\dfrac{6}{20}=\dfrac{3}{10}$$

Fractions can be divided
- ➤ Just flip the second fraction over and multiply as above.

$$\dfrac{2}{5}\div\dfrac{3}{4}=\dfrac{2}{5}\bullet\dfrac{4}{3}=\dfrac{8}{15}$$

Add and subtract the following:

$$\dfrac{7}{8}+\dfrac{5}{16}=$$

$$\dfrac{3}{8}+\dfrac{7}{12}=$$

$$\dfrac{1}{10}-\dfrac{1}{100}=$$

$$\dfrac{3}{5}-\dfrac{9}{10}=$$

Multiply and divide the following:

$$\dfrac{1}{2}\bullet\dfrac{5}{7}=$$

$$\dfrac{4}{7}\bullet\dfrac{6}{5}=$$

$$\dfrac{1}{10}\div\dfrac{1}{100}=$$

$$\dfrac{21}{40}\div\dfrac{7}{8}=$$

©Jantzi Test Prep, Inc.
4actprep.com

NOTES

©Jantzi Test Prep, Inc.
4actprep.com

MANIPULATING FRACTIONS

To add or subtract fractions, you must find a common denominator (bottom).

1. $\dfrac{1}{8} - \dfrac{1}{2}$

2. $1\dfrac{1}{4} + 3\dfrac{3}{8}$

To multiply fractions, multiply numerators (tops) and denominators (bottoms).

3. $\dfrac{1}{2} \cdot \dfrac{1}{2}$

4. $\dfrac{1}{27} \cdot \dfrac{1}{3}$

To divide fractions, flip the fraction you are <u>dividing by</u> and multiply.

5. $\dfrac{\frac{1}{4}}{\frac{1}{4}}$

6. $\dfrac{2}{\frac{2}{5}}$

7. $\dfrac{2\frac{3}{4}}{4\frac{1}{3}}$

To compare two fractions, find a common denominator.

8. Which is larger $\dfrac{5}{100}$ or $\dfrac{4}{80}$?

Practice Problems

9. $\dfrac{\frac{4}{5}}{\frac{1}{3}}$

10. $\dfrac{1}{2} \cdot \dfrac{5}{6}$

11. $\dfrac{\frac{3}{8}}{\frac{1}{2}}$

12. $\dfrac{\frac{3}{11}}{\frac{4}{6}}$

13. $\dfrac{5}{9} \cdot \dfrac{2}{5}$

14. $\dfrac{7}{8} - \dfrac{5}{24}$

15. $2\dfrac{3}{4} \cdot 1\dfrac{1}{3}$

16. $\dfrac{1}{10} - \dfrac{9}{16}$

17. $4\dfrac{2}{8} + 1\dfrac{1}{5}$

18. $\dfrac{3}{14} + \dfrac{13}{32}$

19. $\dfrac{5}{3\frac{2}{9}}$

20. $\dfrac{\frac{4}{5}}{2}$

©Jantzi Test Prep, Inc.
4actprep.com

NOTES

©Jantzi Test Prep, Inc.
4actprep.com

JANTZI ™
☑ T E S T   P R E P

ALGEBRA EXERCISES

A. *Multiplying and Exponents*
Simplify.

1. $x^6 \gamma\, x^2$
2. $(x^2 y)(xy^7)$
3. $3x^8(2x)$
4. $4x(-2x^4)$
5. $3x^7(2x^2 - 4x + 2)$
6. $-x(2x^4 - 2x + 2)$
7. $(x - 1)(2x + 4)$
8. $(x + 1)(7x^2 + 4)$
9. $10(2x + 3y - 5x)$
10. $(x + y)(2y + 5x)$

B. *Combining Like Terms*
Simplify.

11. $(2x^2 + 4x + 2) + (2x - 3) - (1 + 2x)$
12. $2x^3 + x - 4x + 7x^6 - x^3 - 1 + 2x^2 + 4$
13. $(6x + 5) - (8x + 15)$
14. $(15x^2 - 6) - (-8x^3 - 14x^2 - 17)$
15. $y^3 + [(y^2 + 1) + (3y - 7)]$
16. $6ab + 2ab^2 + 3ab + 2a^2 b + 4ab^2$

C. *Division with Exponents*
Simplify.

17. $\dfrac{12x^3 y^3}{3x}$
18. $\dfrac{-14x^3 z^3}{8xy^2 z^2}$

19. $\dfrac{6m^3 n^2}{2m}$
20. $\dfrac{24a^3 b^2 c^2}{3a^2 c}$

D. *Factoring/Distributing*
Simplify.

21. $8x + 24$
22. $\dfrac{10x - 60}{4}$

23. $\dfrac{(x + y)}{y}$
24. $5(x + y) + 2(x + y)$

25. $p(r + s) + q(r + s)$
26. $x^2 - y^2$
27. $x^2 + 2xy + y^2$
28. $3x + 9y + 12z$

©Jantzi Test Prep, Inc.
4actprep.com

NOTES

©Jantzi Test Prep, Inc.
4actprep.com

MATH VOCAB REVIEW

1. Product – The number resulting from multiplying together two or more numbers.

2. Sum – Total amount found by adding two or more numbers.

3. Difference – Total amount found by subtracting two or more numbers.

4. Remainder – What is left over after a number does not divide into another equally in a division problem.

5. Integers – Any negative or positive whole number including zero. (no fractions, ex: -2, 0, 2, 5, 17).

6. Fraction – A division problem.

7. Ratio – A vertically challenged fraction. (3:2)

8. Decimal – A fraction written exactly like money. (½ = .50 = 50 cents)

9. Prime numbers – Any number whose only factors are 1 and itself. (1, 3, 5, 7, 11, 13, 17, 19, 23…)

10. Factors – Set(s) of numbers used to produce a certain product.

11. Average or arithmetic mean – Sum of numbers divided by the total of numbers added.

12. Median – The <u>middle number</u> in a set of numbers arranged in order of size.

13. Mode – The number that occurs <u>most often</u> in a set of numbers.

14. Place value – The value of the location of a digit in a numeral.

15. Right triangle – Any triangle with a 90 degree angle.

16. Isosceles triangle – Triangle with 2 equal sides; base angles are equal.

17. Equilateral triangle – Triangle with 3 equal sides; all angles are equal. (60 degrees)

18. Area – The amount of space in an object found by <u>multiplying</u> side lengths.

19. Perimeter – Distance around a figure found by <u>adding</u> the lengths of all of the sides.

20. Circumference – Perimeter of a circle, but you can't get it by adding.

21. Radius – Distance from center to the circumference of a circle.

22. Diameter - Length of a straight line passing through the center of a circle.

23. Volume – The amount of space occupied by a three-dimensional figure as measured in cubic units. (L x W x H)

24. Parallel – Two lines with equal distance between them that never touch one another.

25. Perpendicular – Line that is intersected by another line at exactly a 90-degree angle.

26. Consecutive – One after another (1, 2, 3, 4…) (Consecutive odd 1, 3, 5, 7…)

27. Numerator – Number on the top of the fraction.

28. Denominator – Number on the bottom of the fraction.

29. Cube – not a square! Three-dimensional shape with six equal square faces.

©Jantzi Test Prep, Inc.
4actprep.com

NOTES

©Jantzi Test Prep, Inc.
4actprep.com

MOST FREQUENTLY USED SAT MATH FORMULAS

Many of the formulas you need to solve the problems on the SAT are given to you on the top of the first page of the math section. However, you will save time if you know many of the most commonly used formulas. Of course, the key is making sure that you know how to **use** each of the formulas listed below.

Area of a circle	$A = \pi r^2$
Area of a parallelogram	$A = bh$
Area of a rectangle	$A = lw$
Area of a square	$A = s^2$
Area of triangle	$A = \frac{1}{2} bh$
Circumference of a circle	$C = \pi d$
Perimeter of a rectangle	Add up all the sides. NEVER MULTIPLY!
Perimeter of a square	Add up all the sides. NEVER MULTIPLY!
Volume of a box	$V = lwh$
Volume of cube	$V = s^3$
Volume of cylinder	$V = \pi r^2 h$
Rate x Time = Distance	An integer is any whole number, including zero. (no fractions, etc.)
Rate x Time x Principal = Interest	A triangle contains 180 degrees. A four-sided figure contains 360 degrees.
Right Triangles Pythagorean Theorem (for all right triangles) 3, 4, 5 and multiples thereof : 5, 12, 13 7, 24, 25 8, 15, 17 $a^2 + b^2 = c^2$ $3^2 + 4^2 = 5^2$ $5^2 + 12^2 = 13^2$	30-60-90 $x, x\sqrt{3}, 2x$ This formula is easy to remember b/c there are 3 different size angles, therefore there are 3 different #'s in the formula. 45-45-90 $x, x, x\sqrt{2}$ This formula is easy to remember b/c there are 2 different size angles, therefore there are 2 different #'s in the formula.

NOTES

©Jantzi Test Prep, Inc.
4actprep.com

JANTZI'S RULES FOR ALL SAT MATH PROBLEMS

1. **Look at the answer choices right after you have read the <u>whole</u> problem <u>carefully</u>.** This gives you an idea of how the answer was written (ie, are the answer choices written in terms of π, as fractions, as decimals, etc?) and also the range of the answers (how big the answers are and how far apart they are from each other).

2. **"BD is your Buddy" can be used if the question is a word problem** with a variable and the answer choices are listed small too big or big too small. If they are big to small, remember you have to go in a different direction.

3. **If there is a diagram, determine if it's drawn to scale (DTS)**. If not, draw your own (DYO).

4. **Always be conscious of the problem number your doing.** Easy questions have easy answers. If you're on an easy question, remember you should not have to go through a long process to get the answer. Look closer – you may have missed something obvious.

5. **See the whole problem at one time to see if there's anything you can see right away.** For example, 2x + 3 and 4x + 6 are related because 4x + 6 is just 2(2x + 3).

6. **Work backwards.** You have the answer choices and a calculator, so if you can't solve the problem the math class way, just plug in the answers to eliminate wrong ones.

7. **When you get in trouble, just look for as many wrong answers as you can, guess, and get out of there!**

8. **Slow down.** When you see words like perimeter, area, circumference, remainder, equilateral, isosceles, consecutive odd, integers, perpendicular, diameter, radius, etc., stop and remind yourself what those terms mean.

9. **If it's a word problem, use "Answer Duh Question."** Read the whole problem first and look at the answer choices. Then read each sentence and don't go on to the next one until you've captured the important information. You may need to write it into an equation.

10. **Get rid of fractions whenever possible.** Multiply everything by the denominator <u>or</u> convert to decimals (money) <u>or</u> plug in 0 for the variable that the fraction is modifying.

©Jantzi Test Prep, Inc.
4actprep.com

NOTES

©Jantzi Test Prep, Inc.
4actprep.com

APPENDIX

©Jantzi Test Prep, Inc.
4actprep.com

NOTES

©Jantzi Test Prep, Inc.
4actprep.com

SMART TALK

This page is an investment in your future. No, that doesn't mean you don't have to read it! *Anyone* can use the most common words in every sentence -- that's the point! If you can articulate on a higher level, you should. People instantly recognize others who use a better vocabulary as more intelligent and therefore, more important. This will equate to a higher salary for these people (OOPS, *I mean individuals!)* Try to use these "upgraded words" in your essay.

COMMON WORD	UPGRADED WORD
Buy	Obtain / Acquire
Luck	Serendipity
Talent/skill	Proficiency
Information	Data
Proof	Evidence
Work	Occupation
Car	Automobile
Rich	Affluent
Poor	Economically Disadvantaged
Bad	Malevolent
Good	Benevolent
Building	Structure / Edifice
Door	Entrance
Drink	Beverage
Fix	Repair
Shine (reflects light)	Luster
Please (make happy)	Gratify
Hatred	Enmity
Start	Commence
Enjoy	Relish
Sneaky	Shrewd
Tell (inform)	Brief
Dull (not sharp)	Blunt
Sharp (pain)	Acute
Criticize	Deprecate
Improve	Ameliorate

©Jantzi Test Prep, Inc.
4actprep.com

NOTES

©Jantzi Test Prep, Inc.
4actprep.com

STUDY SHEET

Directions: Write one sentence summarizing each concept and when it is used.

TQTA/EQEA

_____

POE

_____

BD is your buddy

_____

Work backwards

_____

Good-witch, Bad-witch, Sand-wich

_____

Decoding

_____

Dull pencils

_____

Answer every question

_____

Drawn to scale

_____

Sentence flows smoothly

_____

$2, 1, 0, -2, \dfrac{1}{2}$

_____

Fractions are funky

_____

©Jantzi Test Prep, Inc.
4actprep.com

NOTES

©Jantzi Test Prep, Inc.
4actprep.com

STUDY SHEET (CONT'D)

Read carefully

_____

Bobby Bubblehead

_____

Context clues

_____

Pythagorean Theorem

_____

Area formulas

_____

Perimeter formulas including circumference

_____

Assembly line

_____

Diffusion principle

_____

Fratios

_____

100% correct

_____

Substitute principle

_____

Common Pythagorean triangles: (Draw and Label two example triangles)

_____

©Jantzi Test Prep, Inc.
4actprep.com

NOTES

©Jantzi Test Prep, Inc.
4actprep.com

'TWAS THE NIGHT BEFORE THE BIG EXAM

1. Make sure you pack everything up the night before (Student Strategy Guide, admission ticket, photo ID, pencils and calculator). Put them in the trunk of your car next to the corpse (a Latin root: corp. - body).

2. Treat the night before the test like a school night and plan to wake up with plenty of time to get to the test site.

3. I suggest you eat what you would normally eat in the morning before leaving for the SAT. Because of the length of the test, you're allowed to bring a snack in with you. Keep in mind that all types of fish, kiwi, apples, blueberries, nuts, walnuts, oranges, peppermints and bottled water are brain foods. DO NOT EAT NutraSweet – it is from the devil!

4. Make sure you have your calculator, several number two pencils (don't forget the Big Pencil), an ID, your ticket, peppermints and bottled water.

5. Leave early enough to leave time to get lost (just in case).

6. Upon arrival, stretch like any athlete would. Pull out some practice material and do some problems in the parking lot (20 minutes).

7. Make sure there is a clock visible that works. If there isn't one, then request one from the person who is administering the test. Don't forget to buy a cheap watch (without an alarm) at Wal-Mart because they won't let you have your phone during the test.

8. If anyone makes any weird noises or body hiccups, slap them first, ask forgiveness later.

9. Have fun, don't worry, just relax and kick butt.

10. Remember Jantzi loves you.

©Jantzi Test Prep, Inc.
4actprep.com

NOTES

©Jantzi Test Prep, Inc.
4actprep.com

SAT Test Day Checklist – Stuff to Bring

1. Admission Ticket

Sign-in to My SAT (at sat.collegeboard.org) and click "Print Admission Ticket"

2. Two No. 2 pencils and a soft eraser for the essay; otherwise the Jantzi Pencil rules the scantron

3. Photo ID

State-issued driver's license or ID

School ID card

4. An Acceptable Calculator

Graphing calculator from math class

NO pocket organizers

You can't have your cell phone on your desk! SO NO CELL PHONE CALCULATORS!

5. A Ghetto Watch From Wal-Mart

Remember you can't use your cell phone. You'll look like a nerd, but it's worth it.

6. A Snack and a Drink in your book-bag for your break

Remember your little bottle of water for dipping during the test. The Jantzi pencil an excellent source of fiber – but it doesn't taste very good!

©Jantzi Test Prep, Inc.
4actprep.com

©Jantzi Test Prep, Inc.
4actprep.com

AFTER SESS. #	HOMEWORK ASSIGNMENT	TIME NEEDED	DUE DATE
1	• Study pages 1-18 in the Student Strategy Guide (SSG). • Obtain a copy of "Taking the SAT" booklet from your guidance office or print one online. • Invite your friends to the next class. • Begin Question of the Day at collegeboard.com.	30 minutes	Sess. # 2
2	• Study pages 19-21 in the SSG. • Invite your friends to the next class. • Write the essay and complete the MC grammar questions in the SAT booklet. • Complete all MC grammar questions in the SSG.	60 minutes	Sess. # 3
3	• Complete worksheets 42-50 in the Student Strategy Guide. • Begin roots pages 51-59 in the Student Strategy Guide.	60 minutes	Sess. # 4
4	• Study pages 61-74 in the Student Strategy Guide. • Study the mathematics review in the SAT booklet.	60 minutes	Sess. # 5
5	• Complete the first regular math section in "Taking the SAT," utilizing all strategies taught. (16 or 20 questions) • Study and complete pages 75-98 in the Student Strategy Guide.	60 minutes	Sess. # 6
6	• Complete SPR math section. (18 questions) • Review all strategies and worksheets in the Student Strategy Guide in the back of the SSG. • Remember to "warm-up" for 10-15 minutes right before you walk into the exam!	60 minutes	Before SAT

©Jantzi Test Prep, Inc.
4actprep.com

NOTES

©Jantzi Test Prep, Inc.
4actprep.com

ANSWER KEY

Page 36
He reported to the police that the thief absconded with a great portion of his master's fortune.

Jantzi overwhelmed himself with his own genius.

Page 37
C
C
D

Page 38
The earth is round, though people once believed it was flat.

Once I realized how easy it is to write in complete sentences by making sure that I had both a subject and a verb, it became an easy task to perform.

Quickly

Even though British companies offer much more vacation time than American companies, there is very little difference in productivity.

When the little boy is tired or overly worried, he usually misbehaves.

Page 61
E

Page 62
7/16 - D
6/18 - C

Page 63
4/8 - D
14/16 - A

Page 64
7/16 - B
14/18 – 1/2
12/18 - 90

Page 66
6. P=20, A=25
7. P=40, A=75
5. P=18, A=$9\sqrt{3}$

Page 69
2.8 – D

3.16 – C
6.16 – B

Page 70
12.18 – 11
6.16 – 30

Page 72
16/18 – D
18/20 – B

Page 76
1.8 – B

Page 77
11/20 – E
15/20 – D
10/16 – D
16/18 – 7/16

Page 78
7/20 – D
11/18 – 4, 8, 12, or 16

Page 79
15/16 – B
19/20 – D

Page 80
15/20 – A
13/16 – C

Page 81
6/16 – D
17/20 – D

Page 82
12/18 – 15
11/18 – 513
1 – 9
2 - $\sqrt{34}$

Page 83
4/ 16 – B

Page 84
7/16 – B
12/20 – C
13/16 – C
16/18 – 1/6

©Jantzi Test Prep, Inc.
4actprep.com

JANTZI™
✓ TEST PREP

NOTES

Passage 1 and 2 notes:
Both Q's last
Passage 1st first

Look at schools who superscore Act

official Act/Sat book

make your own answers A

words for knowing:

- But
- Never
- always
- sometimes
- may/might
- however
- although
- Therefor
- Never the less
- maybe
- acctualy
- surprisingly
- while
- whereas
- most
- just
- merely
- simply
- Even

Time words

- First
- last
- before
- after
- still

©Jantzi Test Prep, Inc.
4actprep.com

JANTZI™
✓ TEST PREP

Page 85
14/18 − 1.20
15/18 − 28
17/18 - 1517

Page 86

Percentage to fractions - 7/10, 17/50, 2/5, 87/100
Fraction to percentage − 50%, 18.18%, 75%, 95%
Decimals to percentages − 36%, 225%, 15%, .5%
Percentages to decimals - .24, .49, 2.0, .08

Page 87
472
47
$xy + xz + xq$, $yz(x + a)$
$xyab + xycd - xyef$
77
$3(x + y)$
$ax(b-1 + cd)$

Page 89
3/4
3
2/5
$2\sqrt{10}$
64
x^5
z^6
$5x^3$
$y^3 + y^4$
16
18
1
8
3
1/6
z^7
8^7
x^9
$1/x^2$
1/27
y^8

Page 90
19/16
23/24
9/100
-3/10
5/14
24/35
10
3/5

Page 91
-3/8
37/8
1/4
1/81
1
5
33/52
equal
12/5
5/12
3/4
9/22
2/9
2/3
11/3
-37/80
109/20
139/224
45/29
2/5

Page 92
1. x^8
2. $x^3 y^8$
3. $6x^9$
4. $-8x^5$
5. $6x^7 (x-1)^2$
6. $-2x(x^4 - x + 1)$
7. $2(x+2)(x-1)$
8. $7x^3 + 7x^2 + 4x + 4$
9. $30(x-y)$
10. $5x^2 + 7xy + 2y^2$
11. $2x^2 + 4x - 2$
12. $7x^6 + x^3 + 2x^2 - 3x + 3$
13. $-2x - 10$
14. $8x^3 + 29x^2 11$
15. $y^3 + y^2 + 3y - 6$
16. $6ab^2 + 2a^2 + 9ab$
17. $4x^2 y^3$
18. $-7x^2 z / 4y^2$
19. $3m^2 n^2$
20. $8ab^2 c$
21. $8(x+3)$
22. $5x/2 - 15$
23. $x/y + 1$
24. $7(x+y)$
25. $(p+q)(r+s)$
26. $(x+y)(x-y)$
27. $(x+4)(x+y)$
28. $3(x+3y+4z)$

©Jantzi Test Prep, Inc.
4actprep.com

math   goes from easy to hard

JANTZI™
☑ TEST PREP
NOTES

Think outside the Box

① neg answers   calc no
Section 3

Sec. 4 calc

① Heart of alg.
② Passport to adv. math
③ Problem solving data analysis

25 min
20 Prob
1m 15sec
6 SPR

35 min
38 Probs
1m 35sec
SPR

1. Word Problems

Strategies

① Timing - skip some!

| 12/20 Section 3 | 26/38 section 4 |

Strat 1.
SKIPPING - 5 on sec 3
          8 sec 4

#2 Backsolving
   · use answers

#3: Eliminating
   · eliminate answers off the
     but is they are wrong

#4 Substitution

5 # Turn english into math

6 # Avoid careless mistakes
   · underline ∠ key words
   · circle
   · show work

7# look for shortcuts

② Backsolving

③ Avoid careless mistakes

④ Look for shortcuts
   Substitution Principle

⑤ Eliminate stupid answers
   Pythagorean triples
   3-4-5
   5-12-13

$(a x + 2)(6x + 3)$ $\sqrt{3}$

$abx + 7ax + 26x$

202
©Jantzi Test Prep, Inc.
4actprep.com

$S = 6.50$

$D = 2.50$

$t = 204 \qquad = 836.50$

$D = 204 - S$

$S = 204 - D$

$(204 - D) + 2.50 = 836.50$

$\times 3 \qquad 6.50 + 2.50(204 - B)$

$6.50 + 2.50$